DATE DUE

GAYLORD			PRINTED IN U.S.A.

D1120263

THE MODERN LIBRARY
OF THE WORLD'S BEST BOOKS

AN ANTHOLOGY
OF LIGHT VERSE

The publishers will be pleased to send, upon request, an illustrated folder setting forth the purpose and scope of THE MODERN LIBRARY, *and listing each volume in the series. Every reader of books will find titles he has been looking for, handsomely printed, in unabridged editions, and at an unusually low price.*

EL CAMINO COLLEGE
LIBRARY

An Anthology of

LIGHT VERSE

EDITED AND WITH AN INTRODUCTION BY

LOUIS KRONENBERGER

PR
1175
K7

808.81
K93

THE MODERN LIBRARY · NEW YORK

4689

COPYRIGHT, 1935, BY THE MODERN LIBRARY, INC.

Random House IS THE PUBLISHER OF

THE MODERN LIBRARY

BENNETT A. CERF · DONALD S. KLOPFER · ROBERT K. HAAS

Manufactured in the United States of America

Printed by Parkway Printing Company   Bound by H. Wolff

INTRODUCTION

It is hardly a matter for regret, but it may be one for surprise, that there is more good serious poetry in English than
good light verse. If poets are born, light verse writers are
not. No trances guide their pens: the freshness and gaiety
we ask of them must be achieved through practice and
drudgery. Even Calverley or Gilbert, should you imagine
they were inspired, must have slowly hammered stone into
fluff; and if they didn't (if the evidence proves, for example,
that the lyrics from *Iolanthe* were composed, like *Kubla
Khan,* in a dream) we had better hush up the fact. It would
be far too misleading. Much better to believe, as is probably
true, that light verse (which hasn't even a guardian Muse)
is a sober, long drawn-out and tantalizing business.

Technically, of course, there is a great deal of excellent
light verse. But the technical side of the matter strikes me as
vastly over-emphasized. Unless the versification is accompanied by substance and mood, the result is in the long run
unhappily hollow. There are ever so many people today, for
instance, who are flawless technicians—clever, ingenious, re-
sourceful; yet but little of their work proves really satisfy-
ing, and it is easy to see why. The stuff they write lacks
temperament, character, charm; you merely admire it. It
seldom makes you feel gayer for having read it, seldom
gives you a glow, seldom is fun to reread. The best light
verse must have *human* qualities, however madly they may
have been reshuffled. Something beyond a corner of our
minds must be affected—whether by sheer nonsense, which

gets its effect beyond the mind, or by wit which floods the mind with an enlarging light, or by warmth or spontaneity or the laughter of the body or a pleasantly sensuous appeal. Obviously the best light verse is also poetry.

To me it seems that the best light verse in the English language was written long ago, in the sixteenth and seventeenth centuries, though it was so often published under a different name that even today it sometimes needs pointing out to us. To establish that fact perhaps I must first say what light verse is—or what at least it is to me. I am not sure that my definition is orthodox. The past fifty years would have us suppose that what chiefly distinguishes light verse is, first, consciously clever versification and, second, consciously achieved gaiety—stuff that is plainly labeled rollicking or roguish or humorous or cute or pretty or coy; stuff which is written toward a definite end and which must never invade the inviolable halls of Poetry. I should guess that when the average person thinks of light verse he thinks of Gilbert or Austin Dobson or Eugene Field or Edward Lear. So far as he goes, of course, he is right; but he goes by no means far enough.

As I see light verse, it is almost entirely a matter of mood and accent; and whatever work has that mood and accent, regardless of its form or its subject-matter or its context, is light verse. The mood is simply one of enjoyment, whether quiet or hilarious, cynical or cordial, simple or complex; the accent is simply one of comedy in its many, various and interpenetrating forms; comedy, perhaps I may add, in the philosophical sense of the word. *Both* the mood and the accent must be present and both must be instantaneously and directly communicated; they must not be won to by dint of patient mental labor. And that is all. For the many modern attributes of light verse are in the final analysis

incidentals. If clever riming, ingenious metrics, smart allu-
sions help to achieve the proper mood and accent, so much
the better; but in themselves they are nothing.

If this be conceded, the reason why so much of our best
light verse was written three centuries ago is not hard to
explain. For in those days poets by the dozen wrote with
pleasure and gusto and from a comic standpoint about sex;
and sex is obviously one of a very few topics that have any
permanent interest for mankind. The approach to sex that
these poets used was perfect for achieving the right mood
and accent: they were at once courtly and downright; they
mirrored with both realism and grace the worldliness of
city life and the high spirits of the countryside; they brought
to their experiences a witty and mobile imagination; for all
their high romantic notions they were shrewd about women
and amused rather than heartbroken over the quick passing
and illusoriness of physical love. And they were not high-
falutin: they knew that though they made love with words,
they made love with their bodies as well. The result, in scores
of cases, was good poetry—and good light verse.

When sexual frankness died out in English plays and
novels, it died out also in light verse; and the relatively
puritanical régime which followed (and became absolute
under Victoria) proved the first of three factors which, to
my mind, have in the long run had a bad influence upon
the light verse tradition. By the beginning of the nineteenth
century sex had become "the fair sex," a respectably gallant
phrase that sums up everything; and in the hands of Praed
and his contemporaries the main emphasis shifted from the
personal to the sociable: *vers de société* in an almost literal
sense caught the limelight. But worse was to follow. In Victorian days "the fair sex" became "milady"; and all the technical skill of the Lockers and the Dobsons fails to save their

work from a certain prissiness and cloying prettification. Dobson (who is bookish as well as prudish) achieved the poetic equivalent of Victorian needlework. There is simply no life in him; he never rollicks and he never runs. His interminable rondeaus and ballades, perfect as so many of them are, all smell of the lamp and taste like marshmallow sauce. And the whole school at the head of which Dobson stands—that school of chaste conceits to milady's eyes, hair, lips, throat and other strictly decorous parts of the body; of fans, furbelows, sugar plums, coaches-and-four and masked balls—has booked most of the reserved seats in the anthologies. Actually a little of it goes a very long way. It is the genteel tradition applied to a minor form of culture, and the genteel tradition must everywhere be flouted if a better tradition is to flourish. It is banal, bodyless, sickeningly sweet, and I have excluded all but the best of it. The best is turned so deftly and so polished that it cannot be ignored.

Today sex has come back into the picture, but so far none of our erotic light verse compares to the best of the old stuff. At bottom most of it is much too sentimental, much too close to self-pity; or it is grimly frivolous with a hard-won, Parker-esque sting in its tail. But the writers of light verse are on the right track, for, aside from nonsense and burlesque, the pleasure of the senses, in their many forms, are what such verse can best concern itself with.

Two other things besides Puritanism seem to me to have done the tradition harm—one is a fetich about technique, the other is journalism. Since Calverley there has been too much of an art-for-art's sake attitude toward light verse. Calverley was, of course, a superb technician, and virtually the founder of the modern school of light verse writing. By succeeding craftsmen he is reverenced today as musicians reverence Bach and poets Milton. But it seems to me that,

except historically, he is over-praised, since much of the time
he is almost as empty as he is flawless; and if we are honest
we must confess that we often admire him more than we
enjoy him. As for his influence, I do not think it has been for
the good. He has put an emphasis upon technique which it
should not have, and his followers have tried to outdo one
another in producing novelty and intricacy of rime, metre,
stanzaic form; so that what we find today is versification
run riot and content gone stale. I still prefer the simple, spon-
taneous old-time touch:

> Much ado there was, God wot,
> He would love and she would not;

or

> If she think not well of me
> What care I how fair she be?

or

> Cupid and my Campaspe played
> At cards for kisses; Cupid paid.

to all the breath-taking tours de force of the school which
Calverley helped to found. For it is only an exceptional
person like Gilbert who can turn technical handsprings and
also be funny.

But of all influences which have overtaken light verse in
the past seventy-five years, that of journalism is the most
disastrous. In putting an end to slipshod workmanship the
best of the newspaper columnists and the best of their con-
tributors have performed an admirable service. But the newspaper column in general, together with the topical magazine,
has done a piece of mischief which can no longer be set
aright: it has totally divorced light verse from poetry. For
one person who chooses subjects of permanent interest and
of a poetic nature—like wine or sex or youth or human ab-

surdities—half a dozen celebrate a newspaper item, a mechanical invention, the opening of a subway, a department store ad, a commercial slogan. The fact that they often employ a prodigious technique upon such topics helps very little. The taint of journalism has grown painfully widespread and in almost every instance a poem is dated, is barren of interest and has sprung a humorous leak before a month is out. In reading thousands of such poems I very often yawned; and I was often hard put to it to find something suitable for inclusion here by poets I genuinely respect and admire.

I have tried to bring together in this book all the shorter light verse in English which seems to me good. Difficulties over copyright, it must be added, have now and then kept me from including things that I liked. I have sometimes been inconsistent to avoid being tiresomely repetitious and, so far as actual merit goes, doubtless certain omitted poems are as good as the included poems they too strikingly resemble. Perhaps I have been inconsistent also in ignoring foreign literatures and yet including a few foreign poems in translation. I can only say that in such cases it was entirely the translation that counted: if an English poet did a good job of Heine or Villon or the Greek Anthology, I grabbed it up. But it was the woeful inadequacy of most such translations that led me, half-way through compiling this anthology, to restrict it to the English tradition. To have attempted to represent all the great foreign writers of light verse would have meant, in nineteen cases out of twenty, to malign them.

I have not paid much attention to a man's reputation: there are well-known writers of light verse (Eugene Field, for one example) whose work impresses me as feeble, and such people I have made no bones about completely ignoring or representing very scantily. I have tried to be governed throughout, not by caprice, but by a definite standard of merit; but it is natural that my own tastes rather than poets themselves should sometimes be the true offender. I can only apologize for this obvious fact and go on in my own way. I know, for example, that I have undoubtedly omitted everybody's favorite poem. Every anthologist does. Perhaps a supplementary volume of *Omitted Favorites* can be compiled some day if, as olden writers used to phrase it, the present book meets with a sufficient measure of popularity and success.

Epigrams in verse have been given a section to themselves, and so have parodies. (I have only included the cream of both, since any ideal representation of either would require a book in itself.) I have isolated these two forms of light verse since, as regards epigrams, I couldn't see sandwiching couplets and quatrains into the text wherever they fell chronologically; and as regards parodies they are sometimes, with all due respect to the reader's intelligence and background, not self-explanatory. To offer a little editorial help is surely permissible, and can shame nobody.

L. K.

NEW YORK, *March*, 1934.

ACKNOWLEDGMENTS

I wish to thank the following publishers and authors for permission to reprint poems on which they hold copyright:

D. Appleton-Century Company: *The Jokesmith's Vacation*, by Don Marquis.

Constable & Co.: *The Uses of Ocean*, by Sir Owen Seaman.

Covici, Friede, Inc.: *An Original Cuss, An Epigram*, by Keith Preston.

Dodd, Mead and Company, Inc.: *Feast on Wine or Fast on Water, Commercial Candor, Ballad of Suicide, Song Against Songs*, by G. K. Chesterton. *Dust*, by Rupert Brooke.

M. A. Donohue & Company, *Horace I, 11*, by Eugene Field.

Doubleday, Doran & Company, Inc.: *Those Two Boys, To a Young Woman on the World Staff*, by Franklin P. Adams. *The Tryst*, by Christopher Morley. *Commissary Report*, by Stoddard King. *Male and Female Created He Them*, by Aldous Huxley.

Duffield and Company: *The Akond of Swat, The Nutcrackers and the Sugar Tongs*, by Edward Lear.

E. P. Dutton & Co., Inc.: *Three Epigrams from Martial*, translated by G. A. Pott and F. A. Wright. *This Way Out*, by Margaret Fishback.

Harcourt, Brace & Company: *Der Brief den du Geschrieben, Furcht nichts, geliebte Seele, The Wise Woman, Owen Seaman*, by Louis Untermeyer.

Harper & Brothers: *The Legend of the First Cam-u-el*, by Arthur Guiterman. *Little Boy Blue*, by Guy Wetmore Carryl.

A. P. Herbert: *He Didn't Oughter, Coals of Fire*, from *Ballads for Broadbrows*.

Henry Holt & Company: *Tired Tim*, by Walter de la Mare.

Houghton, Mifflin and Company: *Caprice*, by William Dean Howells. *Good and Bad Luck*, by John Hay. *It's a Fib*, by Elspeth.

Alfred A. Knopf, Inc.: *Poems*, by Bert Leston Taylor. *If You*

Stick a Stock of Liquor, Carmen, The Belle of the Balkans, by Newman Levy.

Rudyard Kipling: *The Ladies,* from *The Seven Seas,* published in America by Doubleday, Doran & Co.

E. G. V. Knox, *To the God of Love.*

Life, *Advice to Worriers,* by George S. Kaufman.

Liveright Publishing Corporation: *Your Little Hands, If You Love Me, Some Folks I Know, The Ocean Spills Upon the Sand, A Little While to Love and Rave,* by Samuel Hoffenstein. *Unfortunate Coincidence, One Perfect Rose, Comment, Résumé, Fable, They Part,* by Dorothy Parker. *The Sisters Kastemaloff, A Royal Pickle, Poem,* by Carlton Talbott. *Meditation,* by Paul Geraldy. Translated by Joseph T. Shipley.

The Macmillan Company: *Ballade of Dead Actors,* by W. E. Henley. *Weathers,* by Thomas Hardy. *Eve,* by Ralph Hodgson. *The Look,* by Sara Teasdale.

Edna St. Vincent Millay: *The Penitent, Sonnet.*

Minton, Balch: *The Tales the Barbers Tell, Drinking Song for Present-Day Gatherings, Ozymandias Revisited,* by Morris Bishop.

The New Yorker: *A Father Does His Best,* by E. B. White.

Joseph Sargent, executor: *How Jack Found that Beans May Go Back on a Chap, The Inhuman Wolf and the Lamb Sans Gêne,* by Guy Wetmore Carryl.

Charles Scribner's Sons: *Behold the Deeds, Shake, Mulleary and Go-Ethe,* by H. C. Bunner. *Infirm,* by Edward Sanford Martin. *A Possibility,* by Carolyn Wells.

Simon and Schuster: *To A Small Boy Standing on My Shoes While I Am Wearing Them, The Oyster, Genealogical Reflection,* by Ogden Nash.

Frederick A. Stokes Company: *I Wish That My Room Had a Floor,* by Gelett Burgess.

The Viking Press: *The Evening Primrose, Ballade of Unfortunate Mammals,* from *Death and Taxes,* by Dorothy Parker.

I should also like to thank Saxe Commins of The Modern Library for his kindness and help.

CONTENTS

CONTENTS

xxiPAGE

CONTENTS

CONTENTS

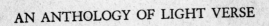

AN ANTHOLOGY OF LIGHT VERSE

Nicholas Breton

THE PLOUGHMAN'S SONG

In the merry month of May,
In a morn by break of day,
Forth I walked by the wood side,
Whereas May was in his pride.
There I spied all alone
Phyllida and Corydon.
Much ado there was, God wot,
He would love and she would not.
She said, never man was true;
He said, none was false to you.
He said, he had loved her long;
She said, love should have no wrong.
Corydon would kiss her then;
She said, maids must kiss no men,
Till they did for good and all.
Then she made the shepherd call
All the heavens to witness truth,
Never loved a truer youth.
Thus with many a pretty oath,
Yea and nay, and faith and troth,
Such as silly shepherds use,
When they will not love abuse,
Love, which had been long deluded,
Was with kisses sweet concluded:
And Phyllida with garlands gay
Was made the Lady of the May.

3

HIS WISDOM

I would thou wert not fair, or I were wise;
I would thou hadst no face, or I no eyes;
I would thou wert not wise, or I not fond;
Or thou not free, or I not so in bond.

But thou art fair, and I can not be wise;
Thy sun-like face hath blinded both mine eyes;
Thou canst not but be wise, nor I but fond;
Nor thou but free, nor I but still in bond.

Yet am I wise to think that thou art fair;
Mine eyes their pureness in thy face repair;
Nor am I fond, that do thy wisdom see;
Nor yet in bond, because that thou art free.

Then in thy beauty only make me wise;
And in thy face the Graces guide mine eyes;
And in thy wisdom only see me fond;
And in thy freedom keep me still in bond.

So shalt thou still be fair, and I be wise;
Thy face shine still upon my cleared eyes;
Thy wisdom only see how I am fond;
Thy freedom only keep me still in bond.

So would I thou wert fair, and I were wise;
So would thou hadst thy face, and I mine eyes;
So would I thou wert wise, and I were fond,
And thou wert free and I were still in bond.

Sir Walter Ralegh

A DESCRIPTION OF LOVE

Now what is love? I pray thee, tell.
It is that fountain and that well,
Where pleasure and repentance dwell.
It is perhaps that sauncing bell,
That tolls all in to heaven or hell:
And this is love, as I hear say.

Yet what is love? I pray thee say.
It is a work on holy-day;
It is December matched with May;
When lusty bloods, in fresh array,
Hear ten months after of the play:
And this is love, as I hear say.

Yet what is love? I pray thee sayn.
It is a sunshine mixed with rain;
It is a tooth-ache, or like pain;
It is a game where none doth gain;
The lass saith no, and would full fain:
And this is love, as I hear sayn.

Yet what is love? I pray thee say.
It is a yea, it is a nay,
A pretty kind of sporting fray;
It is a thing will soon away;
Then take the vantage while you may:
And this is love, as I hear say.

Yet what is love? I pray thee show.
A thing that creeps, it cannot go;
A prize that passeth to and fro;
A thing for one, a thing for mo;

And he that proves must find it so:
And this is love, sweet friend, I trow.

*

DULCINA

As at noon Dulcina rested
    In her sweet and shady bower;
Came a shepherd, and requested
    In her lap to sleep an hour.
        But from her look
        A wound he took
    So deep, that for a further boon
        The nymph he prays.
        Whereto she says,
    Forgo me now, come to me soon.

But in vain she did conjure him
    To depart her presence so;
Having a thousand tongues to allure him,
    And but one to bid him go:
        Where lips invite,
        And eyes delight,
    And cheeks, as fresh as rose in June,
        Persuade delay;
        What boots, she say,
    Forgo me now, come to me soon?

He demands what time for pleasure
    Can there be more fit than now:
She says, night gives loves that leisure,
    Which the day can not allow.
        He says, the sight
        Improves delight.

Which she denies: Nights mirky noon
  In Venus' plays
  Makes bold, she says;
Forgo me now, come to me soon.

But what promise or profession
  From his hands could purchase scope?
Who would sell the sweet possession
  Of such beauty for a hope?
    Or for the sight
    Of lingering night
Forgo the present joys of noon?
    Though ne'er so fair
    Her speeches were,
Forgo me now, come to me soon.

How, at last, agreed these loves?
  She was fair, and he was young:
The tongue may tell what th' eye discovers:
  Joys unseen are never sung.
    Did she consent,
    Or he relent:
Accepts he night, or grants she noon;
    Left he her a maid,
    Or not; she said
Forgo me now, come to me soon.

Anonymous

PHILON THE SHEPHERD—HIS SONG

While that the sun with his beams hot,
  Scorchèd the fruits in vale and mountain:
Philon, the shepherd, late forgot,
  Sitting beside a crystal fountain.

In shadow of a green oak tree,
Upon his pipe this song played he:
Adieu, Love, adieu, Love, untrue Love!
Untrue Love, untrue Love, adieu, Love!
Your mind is light, soon lost for new love.

So long as I was in your sight,
    I was your heart, your soul, your treasure;
And evermore you sobbed and sighed,
    Burning in flames beyond all measure:
        Three days endured your love to me:
        And it was lost in other three.
Adieu, Love, adieu, Love, untrue Love!
Untrue Love, untrue Love, adieu, Love!
Your mind is light, soon lost, for new love.

Another shepherd you did see,
    To whom your heart was soon enchainèd:
Full soon your love was leapt from me,
    Full soon my place he had obtainèd.
        Soon came a third your love to win,
        And we were out and he was in.
Adieu, Love, adieu, Love, untrue Love!
Untrue Love, untrue Love, adieu, Love!
Your mind is light, soon lost for new love.

Sure you have made me passing glad
    That you your mind so soon removèd,
Before that I the leisure had,
    To choose you for my best-beloved:
        For all your love was past and done,
        Two days before it was begun.
    Adieu, Love, adieu, Love, untrue Love!
Untrue Love, untrue Love, adieu, Love!
Your mind is light, soon lost for new love.

Sir Philip Sidney

TRUE LOVE

My true love hath my heart and I have his,
    By just exchange one for another given;
I hold his dear, and mine he cannot miss,
    There never was a better bargain driven.
       My true love hath my heart and I have his.

His heart in me keeps him and me in one,
    My heart in him his thoughts and senses guides;
He loves my heart, for once it was his own,
    I cherish his, because in me it bides.
       My true love hath my heart and I have his.

John Lyly

A SERVING MEN'S SONG

Granichus.   O! for a bowl of fat Canary,
          Rich Palermo, sparkling Sherry,
          Some nectar else, from Juno's dairy;
          O! these draughts would make us merry.

Psyllus.   O! for a wench (I deal in faces,
          And in other daintier things);
          Tickled am I with her embraces,
          Fine dancing in such fairy rings.

Manes.   O! for a plump fat leg of mutton,
          Veal, lamb, capon, pig, and coney;
          None is happy but a glutton,
          None an ass but who wants money.

Chorus.   Wines (indeed) and girls are good,
            But brave victuals feast the blood;
            For wenches, wine, and lusty cheer,
            Jove would leap down to surfeit here.

*

SONG OF APELLES

Cupid and my Campaspe played
At cards for kisses; Cupid paid;
He stakes his quiver, bow, and arrows,
His mother's doves, and team of sparrows;
Loses them too; then, down he throws
The coral of his lip, the rose
Growing on 's cheek (but none knows how);
With these, the crystal of his brow,
And then the dimple of his chin:
All these did my Campaspe win.
At last, he set her both his eyes;
She won, and Cupid blind did rise.
   O Love! has she done this to thee?
   What shall (alas!) become of me?

Thomas Lodge

ROSALIND'S MADRIGAL

Love in my bosom like a bee
   Doth suck his sweet;
Now with his wings he plays with me,
   Now with his feet.
Within mine eyes he makes his nest,
His bed amidst my tender breast;
My kisses are his daily feast,

And yet he robs me of my rest.
    Ah, wanton, will ye?

And if I sleep, then percheth he
    With pretty flight,
And makes his pillow of my knee
    The livelong night.
Strike I my lute, he tunes the string;
He music plays if so I sing;
He lends me every lovely thing;
Yet cruel he my heart doth sting.
    Whist, wanton, still ye!

Else I with roses every day
    Will whip you hence,
And bind you, when you long to play,
    For your offence.
I'll shut mine eyes to keep you in,
I'll make you fast it for your sin,
I'll count your power not worth a pin.
Alas! what hereby shall I win
    If he gainsay me?

What if I beat the wanton boy
    With many a rod?
He will repay me with annoy,
    Because a god.
Then sit thou safely on my knee,
And let thy bower my bosom be;
Lurk in mine eyes, I like of thee.
O Cupid, so thou pity me,
    Spare not, but play thee!

A BLITH AND BONNY COUNTRY LASS

1. A blith and bonny Country Lass
Sat sighing on the tender Grass,
  And weeping said, will none come woo her?
A dapper Boy, a lither Swain,
That had a mind her love to gain,
  With smiling looks straight came unto her.

2. When as the wanton Girl espied
The means to make herself a Bride,
  She simmer'd much like bonny Nell.
The Swain that saw her very kind,
His arms about her body twin'd,
  And said, Fair Lass, how fare ye, well?

3. The Country Lass said, Well forsooth,
But that I have a longing tooth,
  A longing tooth, that makes me cry.
Alas, says he, what gars thy grief?
A wound, says she, without relief,
  I fear that I a Maid shall die.

4. If that be all, the Shepherd said,
I'll make thee Wive it, gentle Maid,
  And so recure thy Malady:
On which they kist, with many an Oath,
And 'fore God Pan did light their Troth;
  So to the Church away they hie.

5. And Jove send every pretty Peat,
That fears to die of this conceit,
  So kind a Friend to help at last:
Then Maids shall never long again,
When they find ease for such a pain:
  And thus my Roundelay is past.

George Peele

SONG FROM *THE OLD WIFE'S TALE*

When as the rye reach to the chin,
And chopcherry, chopcherry ripe within,
Strawberries swimming in the cream,
And school-boys playing in the stream;
    Then O, then O, then O my true love said,
      Till that time come again,
   She could not live a maid.

Henry Chettle

AELIANA'S DITTY

Trust not his wanton tears,
  Lest they beguile ye;
Trust not his childish sight,
  He breatheth slily.
Trust not his touch,
  His feeling may defile ye;
Trust nothing that he doth,
  The wag is wily.
If you suffer him to prate,
You will rue it over late;
  Beware of him, for he is witty.
Quickly strive the boy to bind,
Fear him not, for he is blind;
  If he gets loose, he shows no pity.

John Dowland

BEHOLD A WONDER HERE

Behold a wonder here:
Love hath received his sight,
Which many hundred year,
Hath not beheld the light.

Such beams infused be
By Cynthia in his eyes,
As first have made him see,
And then have made him wise.

Love now no more will weep
For them that laugh the while,
Nor wake for them that sleep,
Nor sigh for them that smile.

So powerful is the beauty
That love doth now behold,
As love is turned to duty,
That's neither blind nor bold.

This beauty shews her might,
To be of double kind,
In giving love his sight
And striking folly blind.

William Shakespeare

FESTE'S SONG FROM *TWELFTH NIGHT*

O mistress mine, where are you roaming?
O! stay and hear; your true love's coming,
    That can sing both high and low.
Trip no further, pretty sweeting;

Journeys end in lovers meeting,
  Every wise man's son doth know.

What is love? 'Tis not hereafter;
Present mirth hath present laughter;
  What's to come is still unsure.
In delay there lies no plenty;
Then come kiss me, sweet and twenty;
  Youth's a stuff will not endure.

*

VER AND HIEMS
Ver

When daisies pied and violets blue
  And lady-smocks all silver-white
And cuckoo-buds of yellow hue
  Do paint the meadows with delight,
The cuckoo then, on every tree,
Mocks married men; for thus sings he,
        Cuckoo!
Cuckoo, cuckoo! O, word of fear,
Unpleasing to a married ear!
When shepherds pipe on oaten straws,
  And merry larks are ploughmen's clocks,
When turtles tread, and rooks, and daws,
  And maidens bleach their summer smocks,
The cuckoo then, on every tree,
Mocks married men; for thus sings he,
        Cuckoo!
Cuckoo, cuckoo! O, word of fear,
Unpleasing to a married ear!

BALTHASAR'S SONG

From *Much Ado About Nothing*

Sigh no more, ladies, sigh no more,
　Men were deceivers ever;
One foot in sea, and one on shore,
　To one thing constant never.
　　　Then sigh not so,
　　　But let them go,
　And be you blithe and bonny,
Converting all your sounds of woe
　Into Hey nonny, nonny.

Sing no more ditties, sing no mo
　Of dumps so dull and heavy;
The fraud of men was ever so,
　Since summer first was leavy.
　　　Then sigh not so,
　　　But let them go,
　And be you blithe and bonny,
Converting all your sounds of woe
　Into Hey nonny, nonny.

Thomas Campion

Turn all thy thoughts to eyes,
Turn all thy hairs to ears,
Change all thy friends to spies,
And all thy joys to fears:
　True love will yet be free,
　In spite of jealousy.

Turn darkness into day,
Conjectures into truth,

Believe what th' envious say,
Let age interpret youth:
    True love will yet be free,
    In spite of jealousy.

Wrest every word and look,
Rack every hidden thought,
Or fish with golden hook;
True love cannot be caught.
    For that will still be free,
    In spite of jealousy!

*

I must complain, yet do enjoy my love;
    She is too fair, too rich in lovely parts:
Thence is my grief, for Nature, while she strove
    With all her graces and divinest arts
To form her too too beautiful of hue,
She had no leisure left to make her true.

Should I, aggrieved, then wish she were less fair?
    That were repugnant to mine own desires.
She is admired, new lovers still repair,
    That kindles daily love's forgetful fires.
Rest, jealous thoughts, and thus resolve at last,—
She hath more beauty than becomes the chaste.

*

Sweet, exclude me not, nor be divided
    From him that ere long must bed thee:
All thy maiden doubts law hath decided;
    Sure we are, and I must wed thee.
Presume then yet a little more:
Here's the way, bar not the door.

Tenants, to fulfil their landlord's pleasure,
    Pay their rent before the quarter:
'Tis my case, if you it rightly measure;
    Put me not then off with laughter.
Consider then a little more:
Here's the way to all my store.

Why were doors in love's despite devised?
    Are not laws enough restraining?
Women are most apt to be surprised
    Sleeping, or sleep wisely feigning.
Then grace me yet a little more:
Here's the way, bar not the door.

Ben Jonson

STILL TO BE NEAT

Still to be neat, still to be drest,
As if you were going to a feast:
Still to be powder'd, still perfum'd,
Lady, it is to be presum'd,
    Though Arts hid causes are not found
All is not sweet, all is not sound.

Give me a look, give me a face,
That makes simplicity a grace;
Robes largely flowing, hairs as free;
Such sweet neglect more taketh me
    Than all th' Adulteries of Art:
They please my eye, but not my heart.

*

FOLLOW A SHADOW

Follow a shadow, it still flies you
 Seem to fly it, it will pursue;
So court a mistress, she denies you;
 Let her alone, she will court you.
  Say, are not women truly, then,
  Styled but the shadows of us men?

At morn and even, shades are longest;
 At noon they are or short or none:
So men at weakest, they are strongest,
 But grant us perfect, they're not known.
  Say, are not women truly then,
  Styled but the shadows of us men?

TO CELIA

Drink to me only with thine eyes,
 And I will pledge with mine;
Or leave a kiss but in the cup,
And I'll not ask for wine.
The thirst, that from the soul doth rise,
 Doth ask a drink divine;
But might I of Jove's nectar sip,
 I would not change for thine.

I sent thee, late, a rosy wreath,
 Not so much honoring thee,
As giving it a hope that there
 It could not withered be.
But thou thereon didst only breathe
 And sent'st it back to me;
Since when it grows, and smells, I swear,
 Not of itself, but thee.

Thomas Heywood

GOOD-MORROW

Pack, clouds, away, and welcome day!
  With night we banish sorrow.
Sweet air, blow soft, mount, lark, aloft
  To give my Love good morrow.
Wings from the wind to please her mind,
  Notes from the lark I'll borrow:
Bird, prune thy wing, nightingale, sing,
  To give my Love good morrow!
    To give my Love good morrow
    Notes from them all I'll borrow.

Wake from thy nest, robin redbreast!
  Sing, birds, in every furrow,
And from each bill let music shrill
  Give my fair Love good morrow!
Blackbird and thrush in every bush,
  Stare, linnet, and cock-sparrow,
You pretty elves, amongst yourselves
  Sing my fair Love good morrow!
    To give my Love good morrow
    Sing, birds, in every furrow!

John Wilbye

LOVE NOT ME FOR COMELY GRACE

Love not me for comely grace,
For my pleasing eye or face,
Nor for any outward part,
No, nor for a constant heart:

For these may fail, or turn to ill,
So thou and I shall sever.
Keep, therefore, a true woman's eye,
And love me still, but know not why—
So hast thou the same reason still
To doat upon me ever!

George Wither

SHALL I, WASTING IN DESPAIR?

Shall I, wasting in despair,
Die because a woman's fair?
Or make pale my cheeks with care,
'Cause another's rosy are?
Be she fairer than the day,
Or the flowery meads in May;
If she think not well of me,
What care I how fair she be.

Shall my heart be grieved or pined
'Cause I see a woman kind?
Or a well disposèd nature,
Joinèd with a lovely feature?
Be she meeker, kinder, than
Turtle-dove or pelican;
If she be not so to me,
What care I how kind she be.

Shall a woman's virtues move
Me to perish for her love?
Or, her well-deservings known,
Make me quite forget my own?

Be she with that goodness blessed
Which may merit name of Best;
    If she be not such to me,
    What care I how good she be?

'Cause her fortune seems too high,
Shall I play the fool and die?
Those that bear a noble mind,
Where they want of riches find,
Think, what with them, they would do,
That, without them, dare to woo:
    And, unless that mind I see,
    What care I how great she be?

Great, or good, or kind, or fair
I will ne'er the more despair;
If she love me, this believe,
I will die, ere she shall grieve;
If she slight me when I woo,
I can scorn and let her go:
    For if she be not for me,
    What care I for whom she be?

Robert Herrick

THE VISION TO ELECTRA

I dream'd we both were in a bed
Of Roses, almost smothered:
The warmth and sweetness had me there
Made lovingly familiar:
But that I heard thy sweet breath say,
Faults done by night, will blush by day:

I kissed thee (panting,) and I call
Night to the Record! that was all.
But ah! if empty dreams so please,
Love give me more such nights as these.

*

CLOTHES DO BUT CHEAT AND COZEN US

Away with silks, away with lawn,
I'll have no scenes or curtains drawn;
Give me my mistress as she is,
Dress'd in her nak'd simplicities:
For as my heart e'en so mine eye
Is won with flesh, not drapery.

*

TO ELECTRA

I dare not ask a kiss;
I dare not beg a smile;
Lest having that, or this,
I might grow proud the while.

No, no, the utmost share
Of my desire shall be
Only to kiss that air
That lately kissed thee.

*

CHOP-CHERRY

1. Thou gav'st me leave to kiss;
   Thou gav'st me leave to woo;
   Thou mad'st me think by this,
   And that, thou lov'dst me too.

2. But I shall ne'er forget,
   How for to make thee merry;
   Thou mad'st me chop, but yet,
   Another snapt the Cherry.

*

A TERNARY OF LITTLES, UPON A PIPKIN OF JELLY SENT TO A LADY

1. A little Saint best fits a little Shrine,
   A little prop best fits a little Vine,
   As my small Cruse best fits my little Wine.

2. A little Seed best fits a little Soil,
   A little Trade best fits a little Toil;
   As my small Jar best fits my little Oil.

3. A little Bin best fits a little Bread,
   A little Garland fits a little Head:
   As my small stuff best fits my little Shed.

4. A little Hearth best fits a little Fire,
   A little Chapel fits a little Choir,
   As my small Bell best fits my little Spire.

5. A little stream best fits a little Boat;
   A little lead best fits a little Float;
   As my small Pipe best fits my little note.

6. A little meat best fits a little belly,
   As sweetly Lady, give me leave to tell ye
   This little Pipkin fits this little Jelly.

THE POET LOVES A MISTRESS, BUT NOT TO MARRY

1. I do not love to wed,
   Though I do like to woo;
   And for a maidenhead
   I'll beg, and buy it too.

2. I'll praise, and I'll approve
   Those maids that never vary;
   And fervently I'll love;
   But yet I would not marry.

3. I'll hug, I'll kiss, I'll play,
   And Cock-like Hens I'll tread;
   And sport in any way;
   But in the Bridal Bed:

4. For why? that man is poor,
   Who hath but one of many;
   But crown'd he is with store,
   That single may have any.

5. Why then, say, what is he
   (To freedom so unknown)
   Who having two or three,
   Will be content with one?

*

DELIGHT IN DISORDER

A sweet disorder in the dress
Kindles in clothes a wantonness:
A lawn about the shoulders thrown
Into a fine distractïon;

An erring lace, which here and there
Enthralls the crimson stomacher;
A cuff neglectful, and thereby
Ribbons to flow confusedly;
A winning wave, deserving note,
In the tempestuous petticoat;
A careless shoe-string, in whose tie
I see a wild civility,—
Do more bewitch me, than when art
Is too precise in every part.

*

TO THE VIRGINS TO MAKE MUCH OF TIME

Gather ye rose-buds while ye may,
   Old Time is still a-flying;
And this same flower that smiles to-day,
   To-morrow will be dying.

The glorious lamp of heaven, the Sun,
   The higher he's a getting,
The sooner will his race be run,
   And nearer he's to setting.

That age is best, which is the first,
   When youth and blood are warmer;
But being spent, the worse, and worst
   Times still succeed the former.

Then be not coy, but use your time,
   And while you may, go marry:
For having lost but once your prime,
   You may forever tarry.

THE GOOD-NIGHT OR BLESSING

Blessings, in abundance come,
To the Bride, and to her Groom;
May the Bed, and this short night,
Know the fulness of delight!
Pleasures, many here attend ye,
And ere long, a Boy Love send ye
Curled and comely, and so trim,
Maids (in time) may ravish him.
Thus a dew of Graces fall
On ye both; Good-night to all.

Thomas Bonham

IN PRAISE OF ALE

When that the chill Charocco blows
    And winter tells a heavy tale,
When pies and daws and rooks and crows
Do sit and curse in frost and snows,
        Then give me ale.

Ale in a Saxon rumkin then,
    Such as will make grimalkin prate,
Bids valour burgeon in tall men,
Quickens the poet's wit and pen,
        Despises fate.

Ale, that the absent battle fights,
    And scorns the march of Swedish drum;
Disputes of princes, laws and rights;
What's done and past tells mortal wights,
        And what's to come.

Ale, that the ploughman's heart up keeps
　　And equals it to tyrants' thrones;
That wipes the eye that fain would weep,
And lulls in sweet and dainty sleep
　　　The o'erwearied bones.

Grandchild of Ceres, barley's daughter,
　　Wine's emulous neighbour if but stale,
Ennobling all the nymphs of water
And filling each man's mouth with laughter—
　　　Oh, give me ale!

Patrick Hannay

A MAID ME LOVED

A maid me loved; her love I not respected;
She mourned, she sighed, nay, sued, yet I neglected:
Too late! too late! alas, I now repent,
For Cupid with her love hath me infected.

As erst he hers, so love my heart now burneth;
As I at her, she laughs at me that mourneth:
Too late! too late! alas, I now repent,
Since her disdainèd love to hatred turneth.

On her alone doth health and hope rely,
Yet still she scorns and doth me love deny:
Too late! too late! alas, I now repent,
Since she joys in my death, I for her die.

Thomas Carew

MEDIOCRITY IN LOVE REJECTED

Give me more love, or more disdain;
  The torrid or the frozen zone
Bring equal ease unto my pain;
  The temperate affords me none:
Either extreme, of love or hate,
Is sweeter than a calm estate.

Give me a storm; if it be love,
  Like Danae in that golden shower,
I'll swim in pleasure; if it prove
  Disdain, that torrent will devour
My vulture hopes; and he's possessed
Of heaven, that's but from hell released.
  Then crown my joys, or cure my pain;
  Give me more love, or more disdain.

Edmund Waller

ON A GIRDLE

That which her slender waist confined,
Shall now my joyful temples bind;
No monarch but would give his crown,
His arms might do what this has done.

It was my heaven's extremest sphere,
The pale which held that lovely deer.
My joy, my grief, my hope, my love,
Did all within this circle move!

A narrow compass! and yet there
Dwelt all that's good, and all that's fair;
Give me but what this ribband bound,
Take all the rest the sun goes round.

*

GO, LOVELY ROSE

Go, lovely rose,
Tell her that wastes her time and me,
That now she knows,
When I resemble her to thee,
How sweet and fair she seems to be.

Tell her that's young
And shuns to have her graces spied,
That hadst thou sprung
In deserts where no men abide,
Thou must have uncommended died.

Small is the worth
Of beauty from the light retired:
Bid her come forth,
Suffer herself to be desired,
And not blush so to be admired.

Then die, that she
The common fate of all things rare
May read in thee;
How small a part of time they share
That are so wondrous sweet and fair.

Sir John Suckling

TO MY LOVE

I pr'ythee send me back my heart,
    Since I can not have thine;
For if from yours you will not part,
    Why then should'st thou have mine?

Yet now I think on't, let it lie;
    To find it, were in vain:
For thou'st a thief in either eye
    Would steal it back again.

Why should two hearts in one breast lie,
    And yet not lodge together?
O love! where is thy sympathy,
    If thus our breasts you sever?

But love is such a mystery
    I can not find it out;
For when I think I'm best resolved,
    I then am in most doubt.

Then farewell care, and farewell woe,
    I will no longer pine;
For I'll believe I have her heart,
    As much as she has mine.

*

WHY SO PALE AND WAN, FOND LOVER?

Why so pale and wan, fond lover?
    Prithee, why so pale?
Will, when looking well can't move her,
    Looking, ill prevail?
    Prithee, why so pale?

Why so dull and mute, young sinner?
   Prithee, why so mute?
Will, when speaking well can't win her,
   Saying nothing do't?
   Prithee, why so mute?

Quit, quit for shame! This will not move,
   This cannot take her;
If of her self she will not love,
   Nothing can make her:
   The devil take her.

*

SHE'S PRETTY TO WALK WITH

She's pretty to walk with:
   And witty to talk with:
And pleasant too to think on.
   But the best use of all
   Is, her health is a stale,
And helps us to make us drink on.

William Cartwright

A SONG OF DALLIANCE

Let not dark nor shadows fright thee;
Thy limbs of lustre they will light thee.
Fear not anyone surprise us,
Love himself doth now disguise us.
From thy waist thy girdle throw:
Night and darkness both dwell here:
Words or actions who can know
Where there's neither eye nor ear?

Show thy bosom, and then hide it;
License touching, and then chide it;
Give a grant, and then forbear it;
Offer something, and forswear it;
Ask where all our shame is gone;
Call us wicked, wanton men;
Do as turtles, kiss and groan;
Say, "We ne'er shall meet again."

I can hear thee curse, yet chase thee;
Drink thy tears, yet still embrace thee;
Easy riches are no treasure;
She that's willing spoils the pleasure.
Love bids learn the wrestlers' fight;
Pull and struggle whilst we twine,
Let me use my force to-night,
The next conquest shall be thine.

John Cleveland

MARK ANTONY

When as the nightingale chanted her vespers,
And the wild forester couched on the ground,
Venus invited me in the evening whispers
Unto a fragrant field with roses crowned,
    Where she before had sent
    My wishes' complement,
    Unto my heart's content
    Played with me on the green.
        Never Mark Antony
        Dallied more wantonly
        With the fair Egyptian Queen.

First on her cherry cheeks I mine eyes feasted,
Thence fear of surfeiting made me retire;
Next on her warmer lips, which when I tasted,
My duller spirits made active as fire.
        Then we began to dart,
        Each at another's heart,
        Arrows that knew no smart,
        Sweet lips and smiles between.
            Never Mark Antony, &c.

Wanting a glass to plait her amber tresses
Which like a bracelet rich deckèd mine arm,
Gaudier than Juno wears when as she graces
Jove with embraces more stately than warm;
        Then did she peep in mine
        Eyes' humour crystalline;
        I in her eyes was seen
        As if we one had been.
            Never Mark Antony, &c.

Mystical grammar of amorous glances;
Feeling of pulses, the physic of love;
Rhetorical courtings and musical dances;
Numb'ring of kisses arithmetic prove;
        Eyes like astronomy;
        Straight-limbed geometry;
        In her art's ingeny
        Our wits were sharp and keen.
            Never Mark Antony
            Dallied more wantonly
            With the fair Egyptian Queen.

Richard Lovelace

THE GLOVE

Thou snowy farm with thy five tenements,
Tell thy white mistress here was one
That called to pay his daily rents;
But she a-gathering flowers and hearts is **gone**,
And thou left void to rude possession.

But grieve not, pretty ermine cabinet,
Thy alabaster lady will come home.
If not, what tenant can there fit
The slender turnings of thy narrow room,
But must ejected be by his own doom?

Then give me leave to leave my rent with **thee:**
Five kisses, one unto a place.
For though the lute's too high for me,
Yet servants, knowing minikin nor base,
Are still allowed to fiddle with the case.

*

TO LUCASTA,
GOING TO THE WARS

Tell me not, Sweet, I am unkind
    That from the nunnery
Of thy chaste breast, and quiet mind,
    To war and arms I fly.

True, a new mistress now I chase,
    The first foe in the field;
And with a stronger faith embrace
    A sword, a horse, a shield.

Yet this inconstancy is such
　　As you too shall adore;
I could not love thee, Dear, so much,
　　Loved I not honour more.

Abraham Cowley

OF DRINKING

The thirsty earth soaks up the rain,
And drinks, and gapes for drink again;
The plants suck in the earth, and are
With constant drinking fresh and fair;
The sea itself (which, one would think,
Should have but little need of drink)
Drinks ten thousand rivers up,
So fill'd that they o'erflow the cup;
The busy sun (and one would guess
By his drunken fiery face no less)
Drinks up the sea; and when he has done
The moon and stars drink up the sun.
They drink and dance by their own light,
They drink and revel all the night.
Nothing in Nature's sober found;
But an eternal Health goes round.
Fill up the bowl then! fill it high!
Fill all the glasses there! for why
Should every creature drink, but I?
Why? man of morals!—tell me why!
　　　　　　(From the Greek of Anacreon)

Andrew Marvell

AMETAS AND THESTYLIS MAKING HAY-ROPES

AMETAS

Think'st thou that this love can stand,
Whilst thou still dost say me nay?
Love unpaid does soon disband:
Love binds love as hay binds hay.

THESTYLIS

Think'st thou that this rope would twine,
If we both should turn one way?
Where both parties so combine,
Neither love will twist nor hay.

AMETAS

Thus your vain excuses find,
Which yourself and us delay;
And love ties a woman's mind
Looser than with ropes of hay.

THESTYLIS

What you cannot constant hope
Must be taken as you may.

AMETAS

Then let's both lay by our rope,
And go and kiss within the hay.

THE MOWER TO THE GLOW-WORMS

Ye living lamps, by whose dear light
   The nightingale does sit so late,
And, studying all the summer night,
   Her matchless songs does meditate;

Ye country comets, that portend
   No war, nor prince's funeral,
Shining unto no higher end
   Than to presage the grasses' fall;

Ye glow-worms, whose officious flame
   To wandering mowers shows the way,
That in the night have lost their aim,
   And after foolish fires do stray;

Your courteous lights in vain you waste,
   Since Juliana here is come;
For she my mind hath so displaced
   That I shall never find my home.

Anonymous

WOULD YOU BE A MAN OF FASHION?

Would you be a man of fashion?
   Would you lead a life divine?
Take a little dram of passion
   In a lusty dose of wine.
If the nymph has no compassion,
   Vain it is to sigh and groan.
Love was but put in for fashion,
   Wine will do the work alone.

DOWN IN A GARDEN

Down in a garden sat my dearest Love,
Her skin more soft and white than down of swan,
More tender-hearted than the turtle-dove,
And far more kind than bleeding pelican.
I courted her; she rose and blushing said,
'Why was I born to live and die a maid?'
With that I plucked a pretty marigold,
Whose dewy leaves shut up when day is done:
'Sweeting,' I said, 'arise, look and behold,
A pretty riddle I'll to thee unfold:
These leaves shut in as close as cloistered nun,
Yet will they open when they see the sun.'
'What mean you by this riddle, sir?' she said,
'I pray expound it.' Then I thus began:
'Know maids are made for men, man for a maid.'
With that she changed her colour and grew wan:
'Since that this riddle you so well unfold,
Be you the sun, I'll be the marigold.'

*

PITY AND LOVE

Pity of beauty in distress
    Should love in me constrain:
Beauty in you should find no less
    Than pity love again:
Your care my curse, your sighs my sorrows prove,
I love with pity, pity me with love.   17

Alexander Brome

I HAVE BEEN IN LOVE AND IN DEBT

I have been in love, and in debt, and in drink,
    This many and many a year;
And those three are plagues enough, one would think,
    For one poor mortal to bear.

'Twas drink made me fall into love,
    And love made me run into debt;
And though I have struggled, and struggled, and strove,
    I cannot get out of them yet.

There's nothing but money can cure me,
    And rid me of all my pain;
        'Twill pay all my debts,
        And remove all my lets;
And my mistress that cannot endure me,
    Will love me, and love me again:
Then I'll fall to loving and drinking again.

NOW I'M RESOLVED TO LOVE NO MORE

Now I'm resolved to love no more,
    But sleep by night, and drink by day;
Your coyness, Chloris, pray give o'er,
    And turn your tempting eyes away.
From ladies I'll withdraw my heart,
And fix it only on the quart.

I'll place no happiness of mine
    A puling beauty still to court,
And say she's glorious and divine,
    The vintner makes the better sport;

And when I say, my dear, my heart,
I only mean it to the quart.

Love has no more prerogative
   To make me desperate courses take,
Nor me t' an hermitage shall drive,
   I'll all my vow to th' goblet make;
And if I wear a capuchoone,
It shall a tankard be or none.

'Tis wine alone that cheers the soul,
   But love and ladies make us sad;
I'm merry when I court the bowl,
   While he that courts the madam's mad:
Then ladies, wonder not at me,
For you are coy, but wine is free.

John Dryden

ROUNDELAY

Chloe found Amyntas lying,
   All in Tears, upon the plain,
Sighing to himself, and crying,
   Wretched I, to love in vain!
Kiss me, dear, before my dying;
   Kiss me once, and ease my pain.

Sighing to himself, and crying,
   Wretched I, to love in vain!
Ever scorning, and denying
   To reward your faithful swain.
Kiss me, dear, before my dying;
   Kiss me once, and ease my pain!

Ever scorning, and denying
   To reward your faithful swain.
Chloe, laughing at his crying,
   Told him that he lov'd in vain:
Kiss me, dear, before my dying;
   Kiss me once, and ease my pain!

Chloe, laughing at his crying,
   Told him that he lov'd in vain;
But repenting, and complying,
   When he kiss'd, she kiss'd again:
Kiss'd him up, before his dying;
   Kiss'd him up and eas'd his pain.

John Crowne

SONG

Kind lovers, love on,
   Lest the world be undone,
And mankind be lost by degrees:
   For if all from their loves
   Should go wander in groves,
There soon would be nothing but trees.

Anonymous

HE THAT MARRIES A MERRY LASS

He that marries a merry lass,
   He has most cause to be sad:
For let her go free in her merry tricks,
   She'll work his patience mad.

But he that marries a scold, a scold,
  He has most cause to be merry:
    For when she's in her fits,
    He may cherish his wits,
  With singing, hey down derry!
He that weds a roaring girl,
  That will both scratch and fight,
    Though he study all day
    To make her away,
  Will be glad to please her at night.
And he that copes with a sullen wench,
  That scarce will speak at all,
    Her doggedness more
    Than a scold or a whore
  Will penetrate his gall.
He that's matched with a turtle dove,
  That has no spleen about her,
    Shall waste so much life,
    In love of his wife,
  He had better be without her.

From New Songs à-la-Mode

*

YES, I COULD LOVE IF I COULD FIND

Yes, I could love if I could find
A mistress fitting to my mind;
Whom neither pride nor gold could move
To buy her beauty, sell her love;
Were neat, yet cared not to be fine,
And loved me for myself, not mine;
Were rather comely than too fair,

White skinn'd and of a lovely hair;
Not ever-blushing, nor too bold;
Not ever-fond, nor yet too cold;
Not sullen-silent, nor all tongue;
Nor puling walk, nor manlike strong;
Modestly full of pleasing mirth,
Yet close as centre of the earth;
In whom you no passion see
But when she looks or speaks of me;
Who calls to bed with melting eyes;
As sweet and fresh as morn, doth rise:
If such a one you chance to find,
She is a mistress to my mind.

Thomas D'Urfey

THE FISHERMAN'S SONG

Of all the world's enjoyments,
 That ever valued were;
There's none of our employments
 With fishing can compare:
  Some preach, some write,
  Some swear, some fight,
 All, golden lucre courting.
But fishing still bears off the bell,
 For profit or for sporting.
Then who a jolly fisherman, a fisherman will be
  His throat must wet,
  Just like his net,
To keep out cold at sea.

The country squire loves running
 A pack of well-mouthed hounds:

Another fancies gunning
  For wild ducks in his grounds:
    This hunts, that fowls,
    This hawks, Dicks bowls,
  No greater pleasure wishing,
But Tom that tells what sport excels,
  Gives all the praise to fishing.
      Then who a jolly fisherman, ...

A good Westphalia gammon
  Is counted dainty fare;
But what is't to a salmon
  Just taken from the Ware?
    Wheat ears and quails,
    Cocks, snipes, and rails,
  Are prized, while season's lasting,
But all must stoop to crayfish soup,
  Or I've no skill in tasting.
      Then who a jolly fisherman, ...

Keen hunters always take to
  Their prey with too much pains;
Nay, often break a neck too,
  A penance for no brains:
    They run, they leap,
    Now high, now deep,
  Whilst he, that fishing chooses,
With ease may do't, nay, more to boot,
  May entertain the muses.
      Then who a jolly fisherman, ...

And though some envious wranglers,
  To jeer us will make bold;
And laugh at patient anglers,
  Who stand so long i' th' cold:

They wait on Miss,
We wait on this,
And think it easy labour;
And if you'd know, fish profits too,
Consult our Holland neighbour.
      Then who a jolly fisherman, ...

William Walsh

THE DESPAIRING LOVER

Distracted with Care,
For *Phillis* the Fair;
Since nothing cou'd move her,
Poor *Damon,* her Lover,
Resolves in Despair
No longer to languish,
Nor bear so much Anguish;
But, mad with his Love,
To a Precipice goes;
Where, a Leap from above
Wou'd soon finish his Woes.

When in Rage he came there,
Beholding how steep
The Sides did appear,
And the Bottom how deep;
His Torments projecting,
And sadly reflecting,
That a Lover forsaken
A new Love may get;
But a Neck, when once broken,
Can never be set:
And, that he cou'd die

Whenever he wou'd;
But, that he cou'd live
But as long as he cou'd:
How grievous soever
The Torment might grow,
He scorn'd to endeavour
To finish it so.
But Bold, Unconcern'd
At Thoughts of the Pain,
He calmly return'd
To his Cottage again.

Matthew Prior

THE REMEDY WORSE THAN THE DISEASE

I sent for Radcliffe; was so ill,
    The other doctors gave me over:
He felt my pulse, prescrib'd his pill,
    And I was likely to recover.

But when the wit began to wheeze,
    And wine had warm'd the politician,
Cur'd yesterday of my disease,
    I died last night of my physician.

*

A TRUE MAID

No, no; for my virginity,
When I lose that, says Rose, I'll die:
Behind the elms, last night, cried Dick,
Rose, were you not extremely sick?

ANSWER TO CLOE JEALOUS

Dear Cloe, how blubber'd is that pretty face?
   Thy Cheek all on Fire, and Thy Hair all uncurl'd
Pr'ythee quit his Caprice; and (as old Falstaff says)
   Let Us e'en talk a little like Folks of this World.

How can'st Thou presume, Thou hast leave to destroy
   The Beauties, which Venus but lent to Thy keeping?
Those Looks were design'd to inspire Love and Joy:
   More ord'nary Eyes may serve People for weeping.

To be vext at a Trifle or two that I writ,
   Your Judgment at once, and my Passion You wrong:
You take that for Fact, which will scarce be found Wit:
   Od's Life! must one swear to the Truth of a Song?

What I speak, my fair Cloe, and what I write, shows
   The Diff'rence there is betwixt Nature and Art:
I court others in Verse; but I love Thee in Prose:
   And They have my Whimsies; but Thou hast my Heart.

The God of us Verse-men (You know Child) the Sun,
   How after his Journeys He sets up his Rest:
If at Morning o'er Earth 'tis his Fancy to run,
   At Night he reclines on his Thetis's Breast.

So when I am weary'd with wand'ring all Day,
   To Thee my Delight in the Evening I come:
No Matter what Beauties I saw in my Way:
   They were but my Visits; but Thou art my Home.

Then finish, Dear Cloe, this Pastoral War;
   And let us like Horace and Lydia agree:
For Thou art a Girl as much brighter than Her,
   As He was a Poet sublimer than Me.

CUPID MISTAKEN

As after noon, one summer's day,
　Venus stood bathing in a river;
Cupid a-shooting went that way,
　New strung his bow, new fill'd his quiver

With skill he chose his sharpest dart:
　With all his might his bow he drew:
Swift to his beauteous parent's heart
　The too-well-guided arrow flew.

"I faint! I die!" the goddess cried:
　"O cruel, could'st thou find none other
To wreak thy spleen on: Parricide!
　Like Nero, thou hast slain thy mother."

Poor Cupid, sobbing, scarce could speak;
　"Indeed, mama, I did not know ye:
Alas! how easy my mistake?
　I took you for your likeness, Chloe."

Jonathan Swift

A GENTLE ECHO ON WOMAN

In the Doric Manner

Shepherd. Echo, I ween, will in the woods reply,
　　　And quaintly answer questions: shall I try?
Echo.　　　　　　　　　　　　　　　　Try.
Shepherd. What must we do our passion to express?
Echo.　　　　　　　　　　　　　　　Press.

．　　．　　．　　．　　．　　．　　．

Shepherd. What most moves women when we them ad,
　　　dress?

Echo.   A dress.
Shepherd. Say, what can keep her chaste whom I adore?
Echo.   A door.
Shepherd. If music softens rocks, love tunes my lyre.
Echo.   Liar.
Shepherd. Then teach me, Echo, how shall I come by her?
Echo.   Buy her.
Shepherd. But what can glad me when she's laid on bier?
Echo.   Beer.
Shepherd. What must I do when women will be kind?
Echo.   Be kind.
Shepherd. What must I do when women will be cross?
Echo.   Be cross.
Shepherd. Lord, what is she that can so turn and wind?
Echo.   Wind.
Shepherd. If she be wind, what stills her when she blows?
Echo.   Blows.

.   .   .   .

Shepherd. Is there no way to moderate her anger?
Echo.   Hang her.
Shepherd. Thanks, gentle Echo! right thy answers tell
            What woman is and how to guard her well.
Echo.   Guard her well.

William Congreve

PIOUS CELINDA

Pious Celinda goes to prayers,
    If I but ask the favour;
And yet the tender fool's in tears,
    When she believes I'll leave her.

Would I were free from this restraint,
  Or else had hopes to win her;
Would she could make of me a saint,
  Or I of her a sinner.

*

SONG

Tell me no more I am deceived,
  That Chloe's false and common;
I always knew (at least believed)
  She was a very woman:
As such I liked, as such caressed,
She still was constant when possessed,
  She could do more for no man.

But oh! her thoughts on others ran,
  And that you think a hard thing?
Perhaps she fancied you the man;
  And what care I one farthing?
You think she's false. I'm sure she's kind,
I take her body, you her mind,
  Who has the better bargain?

*

A NYMPH AND A SWAIN

A nymph and a swain to Apollo once prayed,
The swain had been jilted, the nymph been betrayed:
Their intent was to try if his oracle knew
E'er a nymph that was chaste, or a swain that was true
Apollo was mute, and had like t' have been posed,
But sagely at length he this secret disclosed:
'He alone won't betray in whom none will confide;
And the nymph may be chaste that has never been tried.'

Samuel Lisle

WHEN ORPHEUS WENT DOWN

When Orpheus went down to the regions below,
  Which men are forbidden to see;
He tuned up his lyre, as old histories show,
  To set his Eurydice free.

All hell was astonished a person so wise
  Should rashly endanger his life,
And venture so far—but how vast their surprise
  When they heard that he came for his wife.

To find out a punishment due to his fault,
  Old Pluto had puzzled his brain;
But hell had not torments sufficient, he thought—
  So he gave him his wife back again.

But pity succeeding found place in his heart,
  And, pleased with his playing so well,
He took her again in reward of his art,
  Such merit had music in hell.

Alexander Pope

ON A CERTAIN LADY AT COURT

  I know the thing that's most uncommon;
    (Envy be silent and attend!)
  I know a Reasonable Woman,
    Handsome and witty, yet a Friend.

  Not warp'd by Passion, aw'd by Rumour,
    Not grave thro' Pride, or gay thro' Folly,
  An equal Mixture of good Humour,
    And sensible soft Melancholy.

'Has she no Faults then (Envy says) Sir?'
  Yes she has one, I must aver:
When all the World conspires to praise her,
  The Woman's deaf, and does not hear.

*

THE QUIET LIFE

Happy the man, whose wish and care
A few paternal acres bound,
Content to breathe his native air
    In his own ground.

Whose flocks supply him with attire;
Whose herds with milk, whose fields with bread,
Whose trees in summer yield him shade,
    In winter, fire.

Blest, who can unconcern'dly find
Hours, days, and years, slide soft away
In health of body, peace of mind,
    Quiet by day.

Sound sleep by night; study and ease
Together mix'd; sweet recreation,
And innocence, which most does please
    With meditation.

Thus let me live, unseen, unknown;
Thus unlamented let me die;
Steal from the world, and not a stone
    Tell where I lie.

Anonymous

SUSANNAH AND THE ELDERS

Susannah the fair
With her Beauties all bare,
Was bathing her, was bathing herself in an Arbour:
The Elders stood peeping, and pleased
With the dipping,
Would fain have steered into her Harbour.

But she in a rage,
Swore she'd never engage,
With monsters, with monsters, with monsters so old and so
    feeble.
This caused a great rout,
Which had ne'er come about,
Had the Elders been sprightly and able.

*

THE VICAR OF BRAY

In good King Charles's golden days,
    When loyalty no harm meant,
A zealous High-Churchman I was,
    And so I got preferment;
To teach my flock I never missed—
    Kings are by God appointed,
And damned are those who do resist
    Or touch the Lord's anointed.
        And this is law, I will maintain,
            Until my dying day, Sir,
        That whatsoever king shall reign,
            I'll be the Vicar of Bray, Sir.

When royal James obtained the crown,
   And Popery came in fashion,
The penal laws I hooted down,
   And read the declaration:
The Church of Rome I found would fit
   Full well my constitution,
And had become a Jesuit—
   But for the Revolution.
      And this is law ...

When William was our king declared
   To ease the nation's grievance,
With this new wind about I steered,
   And swore to him allegiance:
Old principles I did revoke,
   Set conscience at a distance;
Passive obedience was a joke,
   A jest was non-resistance.
      And this is law ...

When gracious Anne became our queen,
   The Church of England's glory,
Another face of things was seen—
   And I became a Tory:
Occasional Conformists base,
   I scorned their moderation,
And thought the church in danger was
   By such prevarication.
      And this is law ...

When George in pudding-time came o'er,
   And moderate men looked big, Sir,
I turned a cat-in-pan once more—
   And so became a Whig, Sir:

And this preferment I procured,
  From our new faith's defender,
And almost every day abjured
  The Pope and the Pretender.
    And this is law ...

The illustrious house of Hanover,
  And Protestant succession,
To these I do allegiance swear—
  While they can keep possession:
For in my faith and loyalty
  I never more will falter,
And George my lawful king shall be
  Until the times do alter.
    And this is law ...

*

MAN, MAN, MAN

Man, man, man is for the woman made,
And the woman made for man;
As the spur is for the jade,
As the scabbard for the blade,
As for digging is the spade,
  As for liquor is the can,
So man, man, man, is for the woman made,
  And the woman made for man.

As the sceptre's to be swayed,
As for Night's the serenade,
  As for pudding is the pan,
  As to cool us is the fan,
So man, man, man, is for the woman made,
  And the woman made for man.

Be she widow, wife or maid,
Be she wanton, be she staid,
Be she well or ill-arrayed,
　　Shrew, slut, or harridan,
Yet man, man, man, is for the woman made,
　　And the woman made for man.

*

GREEN BROOM

There was an old man lived out in the wood,
　　His trade was a-cutting of Broom, green Broom;
He had but one son without thrift, without good,
　　Who lay in his bed till 'twas noon, bright noon.

The old man awoke, one morning and spoke,
　　He swore he would fire the room, that room,
If his John would not rise and open his eyes,
　　And away to the wood to cut Broom, green Broom,

So Johnny arose, and he slipped on his clothes,
　　And away to the wood to cut Broom, green Broom,
He sharpened his knives, for once he contrives
　　To cut a great bundle of Broom, green Broom.

When Johnny passed under a lady's fine house,
　　Passed under a lady's fine room, fine room,
She called to her maid, "Go fetch me," she said,
　　"Go fetch me the boy that sells Broom, green Broom."

When Johnny came in to the lady's fine house,
　　And stood in the lady's fine room, fine room;
"Young Johnny," she said, "will you give up your trade,
　　And marry a lady in bloom, full bloom?"

Johnny gave his consent, and to church they both went,
  And he wedded the lady in bloom, full bloom,
At market and fair, all folks do declare,
  There is none like the Boy that sold Broom, green Broom.

*

CHARLIE HE'S MY DARLING

An' Charlie he's my darling,
  My darling, my darling!
Charlie he's my darling,
  The young Chevalier!

'Twas on a Monday morning,
  Right early in the year,
That Charlie cam' to our town,
  The young Chevalier!

As he was walking up the street,
  The city for to view,
O, there he spied a bonnie lass
  The window lookin' through.

Sae light's he jimpèd up the stair,
  An' tirlèd at the pin;
An' wha sae ready as hersel
  To let the laddie in?

He set his Jenny on his knee,
  A' in his Highland dress;
For brawlie weel he kenned the way
  To please a lassie best.

It's up yon heathery mountain,
  An' down yon scroggy glen,
We daur na gang a-milking
  For Charlie an' his men!

An' Charlie he's my darling,
  My darling, my darling!
Charlie he's my darling,
  The young Chevalier!

Oliver Goldsmith

ON THE DEATH OF A MAD DOG

Good people all, of every sort,
  Give ear unto my song;
And if you find it wondrous short—
  It cannot hold you long.

In Islington there was a Man,
  Of whom the world might say,
That still a godly race he ran—
  Whene'er he went to pray.

A kind and gentle heart he had,
  To comfort friends and foes:
The naked every day he clad—
  When he put on his clothes.

And in that town a Dog was found,
  As many dogs there be,
Both mongrel, puppy, whelp, and hound,
  And curs of low degree.

This Dog and Man at first were friends;
  But when a pique began,
The Dog to gain some private ends,
  Went mad, and bit the Man.

Around from all the neighboring streets
  The wondering neighbors ran,

And swore the Dog had lost his wits,
　　To bite so good a Man!

But soon a wonder came to light,
　　That show'd the rogues they lied:—
The Man recover'd from the bite,
　　The Dog it was that died!

Charles Dalmon

EARLY MORNING MEADOW SONG

Now some may drink old vintage wine
　　To ladies gowned with rustling silk,
But we will drink to dairymaids,
　　And drink to them in rum and milk—
O, it's up in the morning early,
　　When the dew is on the grass,
And St. John's bell rings for matins,
　　And St. Mary's rings for mass!

The merry skylarks soar and sing,
　　And seem to Heaven very near—
Who knows what blessed inns they see,
　　What holy drinking songs they hear?
O, it's up in the morning early,
　　When the dew is on the grass,
And St. John's bell rings for matins,
　　And St. Mary's rings for mass!

The mushrooms may be priceless pearls
　　A queen has lost beside the stream;
But rum is melted rubies when
　　It turns the milk to golden cream!

O, it's up in the morning early,
    When the dew is on the grass,
And St. John's bell rings for matins,
    And St. Mary's rings for mass!

Richard Brinsley Sheridan

HERE'S TO THE MAIDEN

Here's to the maiden of bashful fifteen;
Now to the widow of fifty;
Here's to the flaunting extravagant quean;
And here's to the housewife that's thrifty:
    Let the toast pass,
    Drink to the lass:
I'll warrant she'll prove an excuse for the glass.

Here's to the charmer whose dimples we prize;
Now to the damsel with none, Sir;
Here's to the girl with a pair of blue eyes;
And now to the nymph with but one, Sir:
    Let the toast pass, etc.

Here's to the maid with a bosom of snow;
Now to her that's as brown as a berry;
Here's to the wife with a face full of woe;
And now to the damsel that's merry:
    Let the toast pass, etc.

For let her be clumsy or let her be slim;
Young or ancient, I care not a feather;
So fill up a bumper, nay, fill to the brim;
And let us e'en toast 'em together:
    Let the toast pass, etc.

THE PLEASING CONSTRAINT

In a snug little court as I stood t'other day,
And caroll'd the loitering minutes away;
Came a brace of fair nymphs, with such beautiful faces,
That they yielded in number alone to the Graces:
Disputing they were, and that earnestly too,
When thus they address'd me as nearer they drew:
"So sweet is your voice, and your numbers so sweet,
Such sentiment join'd with such harmony meet;
Each note which you raise finds its way to our hearts,
Where Cupid engraves it wi' the point of his darts:
But oh! by these strains, which so deeply can pierce,
Inform us for whom you intended your verse;
'Tis for her, she affirms—I maintain 'tis for me—
And we often pull caps in asserting our plea."

   "Why, ladies," cried I, "you're both handsome, 'tis true,
But cease your dispute, I love neither of you;
My life on another dear creature depends;
Her I hasten to visit:—so kiss and be friends."
"Oh, ho!" said they, "now you convince us quite clear,
For no pretty woman lives anywhere here—
That's plainly a sham. Now, to humour us both,
You shall swear you love neither; so come, take your oath."

   I laughingly replied, " 'Tis tyrannical dealing
To make a man swear, when 'tis plain he's not willing."

   "Why, friend, we've long sought thy fair person to seize;
And think you we'll take such excuses as these?
No, 'twas chance brought you hither, and here you shall
     stay;—
Help, Phaedra! to hold, or he'll sure get away."

Thus spoken, to keep me between 'em they tried;
'Twas a pleasing constraint, and I gladly complied.
If I struggled, 'twas to make 'em imprison me more,
And strove—but for shackles more tight than before;
But think not I'll tell how the minutes were spent;
You may think what you please—but they both were content.

Aristaenetus (358 A.D.)

Richard Brinsley Sheridan and Mr. Halhed, translators

Anonymous

A TOAST

Here's to ye absent Lords, may they
Long in a foreign country stay
Drinking at other ladies' boards
The health of other absent Lords.

*

LET MINIONS MARSHAL EVERY HAIR

Let minions marshal every hair,
    And in a lover's lock delight,
And artificial colours wear:
    Pure wine is native red and white.

Some men want youth, and others health,
    Some want a wife, and some a punk,
Some men want wit, and others wealth,
    But they want nothing that are drunk.

Old Song

Robert Burns

GREEN GROW THE RASHES, O!

There's nought but care on ev'ry han';
   In ev'ry hour that passes, O;
What signifies the life o' man,
   And 'twere na for the lasses, O!

Chorus—

   Green grow the rashes, O;
   Green grow the rashes, O;
The sweetest hours that e'er I spend,
Are spent amang the lasses, O.

The war'ly race may riches chase,
   An' riches still may fly them, O;
An' tho' at last they catch them fast,
   Their hearts can ne'er enjoy them, O.

But gie me a cannie hour at e'en,
   My arms about my dearie, O;
An' war'ly cares an' war'ly men
   May a' gae tapsalteerie, O!

For you sae douce, ye sneer at this;
   Ye're nought but senseless asses, O:
The wisest man that warl' e'er saw,
   He dearly lov'd the lasses, O.

Auld Nature swears, the lovely dears
   Her noblest work she classes, O:
Her prentice han' she try'd on man,
   And then she made the lasses, O.

TAM GLEN

My heart is a-breaking, dear tittie,
   Some counsel unto me come len',
To anger them a' is a pity,
   But what will I do wi' Tam Glen?

I'm thinking, wi' sic a braw fellow
   In poortith I might mak a fen';
What care I in riches to wallow,
   If I maunna marry Tam Glen?

There's Lowrie the laird o' Dumeller,
   'Guid-day to you,' brute! he comes ben;
He brags and he blaws o' his siller,
   But when will he dance like Tam Glen?

My minnie does constantly deave me,
   And bids me beware o' young men;
They flatter, she says, to deceive me;
   But wha can think sae o' Tam Glen?

My daddie says, gin I'll forsake him,
   He'll gie me guid hunder marks ten;
But, if it's ordain'd I maun take him,
   O wha will I get but Tam Glen?

Yestreen at the Valentines' dealing,
   My heart to my mou gied a sten,
For thrice I drew ane without failing,
   And thrice it was written, Tam Glen.

The last Halloween I was waukin
   My droukit sark-sleeve, as ye ken,
His likeness cam up the house staukin,
   And the very grey breeks o' Tam Glen!

Come, counsel, dear tittie, don't tarry;
　　I'll gie you my bonnie black hen,
Gif ye will advise me to marry
　　The lad I lo'e dearly, Tam Glen.

*

THE JOLLY BEGGARS

See! the smoking bowl before us,
　　Mark our jovial ragged ring!
Round and round take up the chorus,
　　And in raptures let us sing:
　　　　A fig for those by law protected!
　　　　　Liberty's a glorious feast!
　　　　Courts for cowards were erected,
　　　　　Churches built to please the priest.

What is title? what is treasure?
　　What is reputation's care?
If we lead a life of pleasure,
　　'Tis no matter when or where.

Life is all a variorum,
　　We regard not how it goes;
Let them cant about decorum
　　Who have characters to lose.

*

EPITAPH FOR JAMES SMITH

Lament him, Mauchline husband a',
　　He aften did assist ye;
For had ye staid hale weeks awa,
　　Your wives they ne'er had miss'd ye.

Ye Mauchline bairns, as on ye press
   To school in bands thegither,
O tread ye lightly on his grass,—
   Perhaps he was your father.

*

DUNCAN GRAY CAM HERE TO WOO

Duncan Gray cam here to woo,
   Ha, ha, the wooing o't!
On blythe Yule night when we were fou,
   Ha, ha, the wooing o't:
Maggie coost her head fu' high,
Look'd asklent and unco skeigh,
Gart poor Duncan stand abeigh;
   Ha, ha, the wooing o't!

Duncan fleech'd, and Duncan pray'd;
Meg was deaf as Ailsa Craig;
Duncan sigh'd baith out and in,
Grat his een baith bleert and blin',
Spak o' lowpin' ower a linn!

Time and chance are but a tide,
Slighted love is sair to bide;
'Shall I, like a fool,' quoth he,
'For a haughty hizzie dee?
She may gae to—France for me!'

How it comes, let doctors tell,
Meg grew sick—as he grew heal;
Something in her bosom wrings,
For relief a sigh she brings;
And O, her een, they spak sic things!

Duncan was a lad o' grace;
   Maggie's was a piteous case;
Duncan could na be her death,
   Swelling pity smoor'd his wrath;
Now they're crouse and canty baith:
      Ha, ha, the wooing o't!

John Quincy Adams

TO SALLY

The man in righteousness arrayed,
   A pure and blameless liver,
Needs not the keen Toledo blade,
   Nor venom-freighted quiver.
What though he wind his toilsome way
   O'er regions wild and weary—
Through Zara's burning desert stray,
   Or Asia's jungles dreary:

What though he plow the billowy deep
   By lunar light, or solar,
Meet the resistless Simoon's sweep,
   Or iceberg circumpolar!
In bog or quagmire deep and dank
   His foot shall never settle;
He mounts the summit of Mont Blanc,
   Or Popocatepetl.
On Chimborazo's breathless height
   He treads o'er burning lava;
Or snuffs the Bohan Upas blight,
   The deathful plant of Java.
Through every peril he shall pass,
   By Virtue's shield protected;

And still by Truth's unerring glass
   His path shall be directed.

Else wherefore was it, Thursday last,
   While strolling down the valley,
Defenceless, musing as I passed
   A canzonet to Sally,
A wolf, with mouth-protruding snout,
   Forth from his thicket bounded—
I clapped my hands and raised a shout—
   He heard—and fled—confounded.

Tangier nor Tunis never bred
   An animal more crabbed;
Nor Fez, dry-nurse of lions, fed
   A monster half so rabid;
Nor Ararat so fierce a beast
   Has seen since days of Noah;
Nor stronger, eager for a feast,
   The fell constrictor boa.

Oh! place me where the solar beam
   Has scorched all verdure vernal;
Or on the polar verge extreme,
   Blocked up with ice eternal—
Still shall my voice's tender lays
   Of love remain unbroken;
And still my charming Sally praise,
   Sweet smiling and sweet spoken.

George Canning

SONG

Whene'er with haggard eyes I view
   This Dungeon, that I'm rotting in,

I think of those Companions true
　　Who studied with me at the U—
　　　　—NIVERSITY of *Gottingen,*—
　　　　—NIVERSITY of *Gottingen.*

> (*Weeps, and pulls out a blue kerchief,*
> *with which he wipes his eyes; gazing*
> *tenderly at it, he proceeds*—

Sweet kerchief, check'd with heav'nly blue,
　　Which once my love sat knotting in!—
Alas! MATILDA *then* was true!—
　　At least I thought so at the U—
　　　　—NIVERSITY of *Gottingen*—
　　　　—NIVERSITY of *Gottingen.*

> (*At the repetition of this Line* ROGERO
> *clanks his Chains in cadence.*)

Barbs! Barbs! alas! how swift you flew
　　Her neat Post-Waggon trotting in!
Ye bore MATILDA from my view.
　　Forlorn I languish'd at the U—
　　　　—NIVERSITY of *Gottingen*—
　　　　—NIVERSITY of *Gottingen.*

This faded form! this pallid hue!
　　This blood my veins is clotting in.
My years are many—They were few
　　When first I entered at the U—
　　　　—NIVERSITY of *Gottingen*—
　　　　—NIVERSITY of *Gottingen.*

There first for thee my passion grew,
　　Sweet! sweet MATILDA POTTINGEN!

Thou wast the daughter of my Tu-
—TOR, *Law Professor* at the U—
    —NIVERSITY of *Gottingen!*—
    —NIVERSITY of *Gottingen!*—

Sun, moon, and thou vain world, adieu,
   That kings and priests are plotting in:
Here doom'd to starve on water-gru—
  —el, never shall I see the U—
    —NIVERSITY of *Gottingen*—
    —NIVERSITY of *Gottingen.*

*

TO MRS. LEIGH UPON HER WEDDING-DAY

While all to this auspicious day
Well pleased their heartfelt homage pay
And sweetly smile and softly say
   A hundred civic speeches;
My Muse shall strike her tuneful strings,
Nor scorn the gift her duty brings,
Tho' humble be the theme she sings,—
   A pair of shooting breeches.

Soon shall the tailor's subtle art
Have made them tight, and spruce, and smart,
And fastened well in every part
   With twenty thousand stitches;
Mark then the moral of my song,
Oh, may your lives but prove as strong,
And wear as well, and last as long,
   As these, my shooting breeches.

And when, to ease the load of life,
Of private care, and public strife,

My lot shall give to me a wife,
   I ask not rank or riches;
For worth like thine alone I pray,
Temper like thine serene and gay,
And formed like thee to give away,
   Not wear herself, the breeches.

Walter Savage Landor

COMMINATION

Taking my walk the other day,
I saw a little girl at play,
So pretty, 'twould not be amiss,
Thought I, to venture on a kiss.
Fiercely the little girl began—
"I wonder at you, nasty man!"
And all four fingers were applied,
And crimson pinafore beside,
To wipe what venom might remain,—
"Do if you dare the like again;
I have a mind to teach you better,"
And I too had a mind to let her.

Thomas Moore

DID NOT

'Twas a new feeling—something more
Than we had dared to own before,
   Which then we hid not:
We saw it in each other's eye,
And wished, in every half-breathed sigh,
   To speak, but did not.

She felt my lips' impassioned touch—
'Twas the first time I dared so much,
    And yet she chid not;
But whispered o'er my burning brow,
"Oh, do you doubt I love you now,"
    Sweet soul! I did not.

Warmly I felt her bosom thrill,
I prest it closer, closer still,
    Though gently bid not,
Till—oh! the world hath seldom heard
Of lovers, who so nearly erred,
    And yet, who did not.

*

THE TIME I'VE LOST IN WOOING

The time I've lost in wooing,
In watching and pursuing
        The light that lies
        In woman's eyes,
Has been my heart's undoing.
Tho' Wisdom oft has sought me,
I scorn'd the lore she brought me,
        My only books
        Were woman's looks,
And folly's all they taught me.

Her smile when Beauty granted,
I hung with gaze enchanted,
        Like him the Sprite
        Whom maids by night
Oft meet in glen that's haunted.

Like him, too, Beauty won me;
    If once their ray
    Was turn'd away,
O! winds could not outrun me.

And are those follies going?
And is my proud heart growing
    Too cold or wise
    For brilliant eyes
Again to set it glowing?
No—vain, alas! th' endeavour
From bonds so sweet to sever;—
    Poor Wisdom's chance
    Against a glance
Is now as weak as ever.

*

WHEN I LOVED YOU

When I loved you, I can't but allow
    I had many an exquisite minute;
But the scorn that I feel for you now
    Hath even more luxury in it!

Thus, whether we're on or we're off,
    Some witchery seems to await you;
To love you is pleasant enough,
    And oh! 'tis delicious to hate you!

Leigh Hunt

THE NUN

If you become a nun, dear,
　A friar I will be;
In any cell you run, dear,
　Pray look behind for me.
The roses all turn pale, too;
The doves all take the veil, too;
　The blind will see the show.
What! you become a nun, my dear?
　I'll not believe it, no!

If you become a nun, dear,
　The bishop Love will be;
The Cupids every one, dear,
　Will chant '*We trust in thee*'.
The incense will go sighing,
The candles fall a-dying,
　The water turn to wine;
What! you go take the vows, my dear?
　You may—but they'll be mine!

*

FAIRIES' SONG

We the fairies blithe and antic,
Of dimensions not gigantic,
Though the moonshine mostly keep us
Oft in orchards frisk and peep us.

Stolen sweets are always sweeter;
Stolen kisses much completer;
Stolen looks are nice in chapels;
Stolen, stolen be your apples.

When to bed the world are bobbing,
Then's the time for orchard-robbing;
Yet the fruit were scarce worth peeling
Were it not for stealing, stealing.

*

JENNY KISS'D ME

Jenny kiss'd me when we met,
　　Jumping from the chair she sat in;
Time, you thief, who love to get
　　Sweets into your list, put that in!
Say I'm weary, say I'm sad,
　　Say that health and wealth have miss'd me,
Say I'm growing old, but add,
　　Jenny kiss'd me.

*

MADAME D'ALBRET'S LAUGH

Yes! that fair neck, too beautiful by half,
Those eyes, that voice, that bloom, all do her honour;
Yet, after all, that little giddy laugh
Is what, in my mind, sits the best upon her.

Good God! 'twould make the very streets and ways,
Through which she passes, burst into a pleasure!
Did melancholy come to mar my days
And kill me in the lap of too much leisure,
No spell were wanting, from the dead to raise me,
But only that sweet laugh wherewith she slays me.
                    Translated from the French of Marot

Thomas Love Peacock

FROM *CROCHET CASTLE*

After careful meditation,
And profound deliberation,
On the various pretty projects which have just been shown,
Not a scheme in agitation,
For the world's amelioration,
Has a grain of common sense in it, except my own.

*

THE WAR-SONG OF DINAS VAWR

The mountain sheep are sweeter,
But the valley sheep are fatter;
We therefore deemed it meeter
To carry off the latter.
We made an expedition;
We met a host, and quelled it;
We forced a strong position,
And killed the men who held it.

On Dyfed's richest valley,
Where herds of kine were browsing,
We made a mighty sally,
To furnish our carousing.
Fierce warriors rushed to meet us;
We met them, and o'erthrew them:
They struggled hard to beat us;
But we conquered them, and slew them.

As we drove our prize at leisure.
The king marched forth to catch us;

His rage surpassed all measure,
But his people could not match us.
He fled to his hall-pillars;
And, ere our force we led off,
Some sacked his house and cellars,
While others cut his head off.

We there, in strife bewild'ring,
Spilt blood enough to swim in:
We orphaned many children,
And widowed many women.
The eagles and the ravens
We glutted with our foemen;
The heroes and the cravens,
The spearmen and the bowmen.

We brought away from battle,
And much their land bemoaned them,
Two thousand head of cattle,
And the head of him who owned them:
Ednyfed, king of Dyfed,
His head was borne before us;
His wine and beasts supplied our feasts,
And his overthrow, our chorus.

*

THE GREY FRIAR

Why are thy looks so blank, grey friar?
    Why are thy looks so blue?
Thou seem'st more pale and lank, grey friar,
    Than thou wast used to do:—
    Say, what has made thee rue?

Thy form was plump, and a light did shine
  In thy round and ruby face,
Which showed an outward visible sign
  Of an inward spiritual grace:—
  Say, what has changed thy case?

Yet will I tell thee true, grey friar,
  I very well can see,
That, if thy looks are blue, grey friar,
  'Tis all for love of me,—
  'Tis all for love of me.

But breathe not thy vows to me, grey friar,
  Oh, breathe them not, I pray;
For ill beseem in a reverend friar,
  The love of a mortal may;
  And I needs must say thee nay.

But could'st thou think my heart to move
  With that pale and silent scowl?
Know, he who would win a maiden's love,
  Whether clad in cap or cowl,
  Must be more of a lark than an owl.

Lord Byron

WRITTEN AFTER SWIMMING FROM SESTOS TO ABYDOS

If, in the month of dark December,
  Leander, who was nightly wont
(What maid will not the tale remember?)
  To cross thy stream, broad Hellespont!

If, when the wintry tempest roar'd,
   He sped to Hero, nothing loth,
And thus of old thy current pour'd,
   Fair Venus! how I pity both!

For *me,* degenerate modern wretch,
   Though in the genial month of May,
My dripping limbs I faintly stretch,
   And think I've done a feat to-day.

But since he cross'd the rapid tide,
   According to the doubtful story,
To woo,—and—Lord knows what beside,
   And swam for Love, as I for Glory;

'Twere hard to say who fared the best:
   Sad mortals! thus the gods still plague you!
He lost his labour, I my jest;
   For he was drown'd, and I've the ague.

Thomas Hood

ALL IN THE DOWNS

I would I had something to do—or to think!
   Or something to read, or to write!
I am rapidly verging on lunacy's brink,
   Or I shall be dead before night.

In my ears has been ringing and droning all day,
   Without ever a stop or a change,
That poem of Tennyson's—heart-cheering lay!—
   Of the moated monotonous Grange!

The stripes in the carpet and paper alike
   I have counted, and counted all through,

And now I've a fervid ambition to strike
Out some path of wild pleasure that's new.

They say, if a number you count, and recount,
That the time imperceptibly goes,—
Ah! I wish—how I wish!—I'd ne'er learnt the amount
Of my aggregate fingers and toes.

"Enjoyment is fleeting," the proverbs all say,
"Even that which it feeds upon fails."
I've arrived at the truth of the saying to-day,
By devouring the whole of my nails.

I have numbered the minutes so heavy and slow,
Till of that dissipation I tire,
And as for exciting amusements,—you know
One can't *always* be stirring the fire.

*

LINES IN A YOUNG LADY'S ALBUM

A pretty task, Miss S——, to ask
A Benedictine pen,
That cannot quite at freedom write
Like those of other men.
No lover's plaint my Muse must paint
To fill this page's span,
But be correct and recollect
I'm not a single man.

Pray only think for pen and ink
How hard to get along,
That may not turn on words that burn,
Or Love, the life of song!

Nine Muses, if I chooses, I
  May woo all in a clan,
But one Miss S—— I daren't address—
  I'm not a single man.

Scribblers unwed, with little head
  May eke it out with heart,
And in their lays it often plays
  A rare first-fiddle part:
They make a kiss to rhyme with bliss,
  But if I so began,
I have my fears about my ears—
  I'm not a single man.

Upon your cheek I may not speak,
  Nor on your lip be warm,
I must be wise about your eyes,
  And formal with your form;
Of all that sort of thing, in short,
  On T. H. Bayly's plan,
I must not twine a single line—
  I'm not a single man.

A watchman's part compels my heart
  To keep you off its beat,
And I might dare as soon to swear
  At you as at your feet.
I can't expire in passion's fire,
  As other poets can—
My wife (she's by) won't let me die—
  I'm not a single man.

Shut out from love, denied a dove,
  Forbidden bow and dart,

Without a groan to call my own,
    With neither hand nor heart,
To Hymen vowed, and not allowed
    To flirt e'en with your fan,
Here end, as just a friend, I must—
    I'm not a single man.

Winthrop Mackworth Praed

THE BELLE OF THE BALL-ROOM

Years—years ago,—ere yet my dreams
    Had been of being wise or witty,—
Ere I had done with writing themes,
    Or yawned o'er this infernal Chitty;—
Years—years ago,—while all my joy
    Was in my fowling-piece and filly,—
In short, while I was yet a boy,
    I fell in love with Laura Lily.

I saw her at the County Ball:
    There, when the sounds of flute and fiddle
Gave signal sweet in that old hall
    Of hands across and down the middle,
Hers was the subtlest spell by far
    Of all that set young hearts romancing;
She was our queen, our rose, our star;
    And then she danced—O Heaven, her dancing!

Dark was her hair, her hand was white;
    Her voice was exquisitely tender;
Her eyes were full of liquid light;
    I never saw a waist to slender!
Her every look, her every smile,
    Shot right and left a score of arrows;

I thought 'twas Venus from her isle,
 And wondered where she'd left her sparrows.

She talked,—of politics or prayers,—
 Of Southey's prose or Wordsworth's sonnets,—
Of danglers—or of dancing bears,
 Of battles—or the last new bonnets,
By candlelight, at twelve o'clock,
 To me it mattered not a tittle;
If those bright lips had quoted Locke,
 I might have thought they murmured Little.

Through sunny May, through sultry June,
 I loved her with a love eternal;
I spoke her praises to the moon,
 I wrote them to the Sunday Journal:
My mother laughed; I soon found out
 That ancient ladies have no feeling:
My father frowned; but how should gout
 See any happiness in kneeling?

She was the daughter of a Dean,
 Rich, fat, and rather apoplectic;
She had one brother, just thirteen,
 Whose colour was extremely hectic;
Her grandmother for many a year
 Had fed the parish with her bounty;
Her second cousin was a peer,
 And Lord Lieutenant of the County.

But titles, and the three per cents,
 And mortgages, and great relations,
And India bonds, and tithes, and rents,
 Oh, what are they to love's sensations?

Black eyes, fair forehead, clustering locks—
    Such wealth, such honours, Cupid chooses;
He cares as little for the Stocks,
    As Baron Rothschild for the Muses.

She sketched; the vale, the wood, the beach,
    Grew lovelier from her pencil's shading:
She botanised; I envied each
    Young blossom in her boudoir fading:
She warbled Handel; it was grand;
    She made the Catalani jealous:
She touched the organ; I could stand
    For hours and hours to blow the bellows.

She kept an album, too, at home,
    Well filled with all an album's glories;
Paintings of butterflies, and Rome,
    Patterns for trimmings, Persian stories;
Soft songs to Julia's cockatoo,
    Fierce odes to Famine and to Slaughter;
And autographs of Prince Leboo,
    And recipes for elder-water.

And she was flattered, worshipped, bored;
    Her steps were watched, her dress was noted.
Her poodle dog was quite adored,
    Her sayings were extremely quoted;
She laughed, and every heart was glad,
    As if the taxes were abolished;
She frowned, and every look was sad,
    As if the Opera were demolished.

She smiled on many, just for fun,—
    I knew that there was nothing in it;

I was the first—the only one
  Her heart had thought of for a minute.—
I knew it, for she told me so,
  In phrase which was divinely moulded;
She wrote a charming hand,—and oh!
  How sweetly all her notes were folded!

Our love was like most other loves;—
  A little glow, a little shiver,
A rose-bud, and a pair of gloves,
  And "Fly not yet"—upon the river;
Some jealousy of some one's heir,
  Some hopes of dying broken-hearted;
A miniature, a lock of hair,
  The usual vows,—and then we parted.

We parted; months and years rolled by;
  We met again four summers after:
Our parting was all sobs and sigh;
  Our meeting was all mirth and laughter:
For in my heart's most secret cell
  There had been many other lodgers;
And she was not the ball-room's belle,
  But only—Mrs. Something Rogers!

*

GOOD-NIGHT TO THE SEASON

"So runs the world away."—*Hamlet*

Good-night to the Season! 'tis over!
  Gay dwellings no longer are gay;
The courtier, the gambler, the lover,
  Are scattered like swallows away;

There's nobody left to invite one,
   Except my good uncle and spouse;
My mistress is bathing at Brighton,
   My patron is sailing at Cowes;
For want of a better employment,
   Till Ponto and Don can get out,
I'll cultivate rural enjoyment,
   And angle immensely for trout.

Good-night to the Season! the lobbies,
   Their changes, and rumours of change,
Which startled the rustic Sir Bobbies,
   And made all the Bishops look strange;
The breaches, and battles, and blunders,
   Performed by the Commons and Peers;
The Marquis's eloquent thunders,
   The Baronet's eloquent ears;
Denouncings of Papists and treasons,
   Of foreign dominion, and oats;
Misrepresentations of reasons,
   And misunderstandings of notes.

Good-night to the Season! the building's
   Enough to make Inigo sick;
The paintings, and plasterings, and gildings
   Of stucco, and marble, and brick;
The orders deliciously blended,
   From love of effect, into one;
The club-houses only intended,
   The palaces only begun;
The hell, where the fiend in his glory
   Sits staring at putty and stones,
And scrambles from story to story,
   To rattle at midnight his bones.

Good-night to the Season! the dances,
   The fillings of hot little rooms,
The glancings of rapturous glances,
   The fancyings of fancy costumes;
The pleasures which fashion makes duties
   The praisings of fiddles and flutes,
The luxury of looking at beauties,
   The tedium of talking to mutes;
The female diplomatists, planners
   Of matches for Laura and Jane,
The ice of her Ladyship's manners,
   The ice of his Lordship's champagne.

Good-night to the Season! the rages
   Led off by the chiefs of the throng,
The Lady Matilda's new pages,
   The Lady Eliza's new song;
Miss Fennel's macaw, which at Boodle's
   Was held to have something to say;
Mrs. Splenetic's musical poodles,
   Which bark "Batti—Batti!" all day;
The pony Sir Araby sported,
   As hot and as black as a coal,
And the lion his mother imported,
   In bearskins and grease, from the Pole.

Good-night to the Season! the Toso,
   So very majestic and tall;
Miss Ayton, whose singing was so-so,
   And Pasta, divinest of all;
The labour in vain of the ballet,
   So sadly deficient in stars;
The foreigners thronging the Alley,
   Exhaling the breath of cigars;

The *loge,* where some heiress, how killing!—
    Environed with exquisites, sits,
The lovely one out of her drilling,
    The silly ones out of their wits.

Good-night to the Season! the splendour
    That beamed in the Spanish bazaar,
Where I purchased—my heart was so tender—
    A card-case,—a pasteboard guitar,—
A bottle of perfume,—a girdle,—
    A lithographed Riego, full-grown,
Whom bigotry drew on a hurdle,
    That artists might draw him on stone,—
A small panorama of Seville,—
    A trap for demolishing flies,—
A caricature of the Devil,—
    And a look from Miss Sheridan's eyes.

Good-night to the Season! the flowers
    Of the grand horticultural fête,
When boudoirs were quitted for bowers,
    And the fashion was, not to be late;
When all who had money and leisure
    Grew rural o'er ices and wines,
All pleasantly toiling for pleasure,
    All hungrily pining for pines,
And making of beautiful speeches,
    And marring of beautiful shows,
And feeding on delicate peaches,
    And treading on delicate toes.

Good-night to the Season! another
    Will come with its trifles and toys,
And hurry away, like its brother,
    In sunshine, and odour, and noise.

Will it come with a rose, or a brier?
  Will it come with a blessing, or curse?
Will its bonnets be lower, or higher?
  Will its morals be better, or worse?
Will it find me grown thinner, or fatter,
  Or fonder of wrong or of right,
Or married, or buried?—no matter,—
  Good-night to the Season!—Good-night!

*

THE TALENTED MAN

A LETTER FROM A LADY IN LONDON TO A LADY AT LAUSANNE

Dear Alice! you'll laugh when you know it,—
  Last week, at the Duchess's ball,
I danced with the clever new poet,—
  You've heard of him,—Tully St. Paul.
Miss Jonquil was perfectly frantic;
  I wish you had seen Lady Anne!
It really was very romantic,
  He *is* such a talented man!

He came up from Brazen Nose College,
  Just caught, as they call it, this spring;
And his head, love, is stuffed full of knowledge
  Of every conceivable thing.
Of science and logic he chatters,
  As fine and as fast as he can;
Though I am no judge of such matters,
  I'm sure he's a talented man.

His stories and jests are delightful;—
  Not stories or jests, dear, for you;

The jests are exceedingly spiteful,
  The stories not always *quite* true.
Perhaps to be kind and veracious
  May do pretty well at Lausanne;
But it never would answer,—good gracious!
  Chez nous—in a talented man.

He sneers,—how my Alice would scold him!—
  At the bliss of a sigh or a tear;
He laughed—only think!—when I told him
  How we cried o'er Trevelyan last year;
I vow I was quite in a passion;
  I broke all the sticks of my fan;
But sentiment's quite out of fashion,
  It seems, in a talented man.

Lady Bab, who is terribly moral,
  Has told me that Tully is vain,
And apt—which is silly—to quarrel,
  And fond—which is sad—of champagne.
I listened, and doubted, dear Alice,
  For I saw, when my lady began,
It was only the Dowager's malice;—
  She *does* hate a talented man!

He's hideous, I own it. But fame, love,
  Is all that these eyes can adore;
He's lame,—but Lord Byron was lame, love,
  And dumpy,—but so is Tom Moore.
Then his voice,—*such* a voice! my sweet creature,
  It's like your Aunt Lucy's toucan:
But oh! what's a tone or a feature,
  When once one's a talented man?

My mother, you know, all the season,
    Has talked of Sir Geoffrey's estate;
And truly, to do the fool reason,
    He *has* been less horrid of late.
But to-day, when we drive in the carriage,
    I'll tell her to lay down her plan;—
If ever I venture on marriage,
    It must be a talented man!

P. S.—I have found, on reflection,
    One fault in my friend,—*entre nous;*
Without it, he'd just be perfection;—
    Poor fellow, he has not a *soul!*
And so, when he comes in September,
    To shoot with my uncle, Sir Dan,
I've promised mamma to remember
    He's *only* a talented man!

Marjorie Fleming

SONNET TO A MONKEY

O lively, O most charming pug,
Thy graceful air, and heavenly mug;
The beauties of his mind do shine,
And every bit is shaped and fine.
Your teeth are whiter than the snow,
You're a great buck, you're a great beau;
Your eyes are of so nice a shape,
More like a Christian's than an ape;
Your cheek is like the rose's blume,
Your hair is like the raven's plume;

His nose's cast is of the Roman,
He is a very pretty woman.
I could not get a rhyme for Roman,
So was obliged to call him woman.

Charles Lever

MICKEY FREE'S SONG

It's little for glory I care;
   Sure ambition is only a fable;
I'd as soon be myself as Lord Mayor,
   With lashings of drink on the table.
I like to lie down in the sun
   And *drame,* when my *faytures* is scorchin'
That when I'm too *ould* for more fun,
   Why, I'll marry a wife with a fortune.

And in winter, with bacon and eggs,
   And a place at the turf-fire basking,
Sip my punch as I roasted my legs,
   Oh, the devil a more I'd be asking!
For I haven't a *janius* for work,—
   It was never the gift of the Bradies,—
But I'd make a most *illigant* Turk,
   For I'm fond of tobacco and ladies.

Lady Dufferin

THE CHARMING WOMAN

So Miss Myrtle is going to marry?
   What a number of hearts she will break!
There's Lord George, and Tom Brown, and Sir Harry
   Who are dying of love for her sake!

'Tis a match that we all must approve,—
  Let gossips say all that they can!
For indeed she's a charming woman,
  And he's a most fortunate man!

Yes, indeed, she's a charming woman,
  And she reads both Latin and Greek,—
And I'm told that she solved a problem
  In Euclid before she could speak!
Had she been but a daughter of mine,
  I'd have taught her to hem and to sew,—
But her mother (a charming woman)
  Couldn't think of such trifles, you know!

Oh, she's really a charming woman!
  But, perhaps, a little too thin;
And no wonder such very late hours
  Should ruin her beautiful skin!
And her shoulders are rather too bare,
  And her gown's nearly up to her knees,
But I'm told that these charming women
  May dress themselves just as they please!

Yet, she's really a charming woman!
  But, I thought I observed, by the bye,
A something—that's rather uncommon,—
  In the flash of that very bright eye?
It may be a mere fancy of mine,
  Tho' her voice has a very sharp tone,—
But I'm told that these charming women
  Are inclined to have wills of their own!

She sings like a bullfinch or linnet,
  And she talks like an Archbishop too;
Can play you a rubber and win it,—
  If she's got nothing better to do!

She can chatter of Poor-Laws and Tithes,
  And the value of labour and land,—
'Tis a pity when charming women
  Talk of things which they don't understand!

I'm told that she hasn't a penny,
  Yet her gowns would make Maradan stare;
And I feel her bills must be many,—
  But that's only her husband's affair!
Such husbands are very uncommon,
  So regardless of prudence and pelf,—
But they say such a charming woman
  Is a fortune, you know, in herself.

She's brothers and sisters by dozens,
  And all charming people, they say!
And several tall Irish cousins,
  Whom she loves in a sisterly way.
O young men, if you'd take my advice,
  You would find it an excellent plan,—
Don't marry a charming woman,
  If you are a sensible man.

Oliver Wendell Holmes

THE HEIGHT OF THE RIDICULOUS

I wrote some lines once on a time
  In wondrous merry mood,
And thought, as usual, men would say
  They were exceeding good.

They were so queer, so very queer,
  I laughed as I would die;
Albeit, in the general way,
  A sober man am I.

I called my servant, and he came;
   How kind it was of him
To mind a slender man like me,
   He of the mighty limb.

"These to the printer," I exclaimed,
   And, in my humorous way,
I added (as a trifling jest,)
   "There'll be the devil to pay."

He took the paper, and I watched,
   And saw him peep within;
At the first line he read, his face
   Was all upon the grin.

He read the next; the grin grew broad,
   And shot from ear to ear;
He read the third; a chuckling noise
   I now began to hear.

The fourth; he broke into a roar;
   The fifth; his waistband split;
The sixth; he burst five buttons off,
   And tumbled in a fit.

Ten days and nights, with sleepless eye,
   I watched that wretched man,
And since, I never dare to write
   As funny as I can.

William Makepeace Thackeray

THE SORROWS OF WERTHER

Werther had a love for Charlotte
   Such as words could never utter;
Would you know how first he met her?
   She was cutting bread and butter.

Charlotte was a married lady,
 And a moral man was Werther,
And for all the wealth of Indies,
 Would do nothing for to hurt her.

So he sigh'd and pined and ogled,
 And his passion boil'd and bubbled,
Till he blew his silly brains out,
 And no more was by it troubled.

Charlotte, having seen his body
 Borne before her on a shutter,
Like a well-conducted person,
 Went on cutting bread and butter.

*

COMMANDERS OF THE FAITHFUL

The Pope he is a happy man,
His palace is the Vatican,
And there he sits and drains his can:
The Pope he is a happy man.
I often say when I'm at home,
I'd like to be the Pope of Rome.

And then there's Sultan Saladin,
That Turkish Soldan full of sin;
He has a hundred wives at least,
By which his pleasure is increased:
I've often wished, I hope no sin,
That I were Sultan Saladin.

But no, the Pope no wife may choose,
And so I would not wear his shoes;

No wine may drink the proud Paynim,
  And so I'd rather not be him:
My wife, my wine, I love, I hope,
  And would be neither Turk nor Pope.

*

THE BALLAD OF BOUILLABAISSE

A street there is in Paris famous,
  For which no rhyme our language yields,
Rue Neuve des Petits Champs its name is—
  The New Street of the Little Fields.
And here's an inn, not rich and splendid
  But still in comfortable case;
The which in youth I oft attended
  To eat a bowl of Bouillabaisse.

This Bouillabaisse a noble dish is,
  A sort of soup or broth, or brew,
Or hotchpotch of all sorts of fishes
  That Greenwich never could outdo;
Green herbs, red peppers, mussels, saffron,
  Soles, onions, garlic, roach and dace:
All these you eat at Terrè's tavern
  In that one dish of Bouillabaisse.

Indeed a rich and savoury stew 'tis;
  And true philosophers, methinks,
Who love all sorts of natural beauties
  Should love good victuals and good drinks.
And Cordelier or Benedictine
  Might gladly, sure, his lot embrace,
Nor find a fast-day too afflicting
  Which served him up a Bouillabaisse.

I wonder if the house still there is?
   Yes, here the lamp is, as before;
The smiling red-cheeked "écaillère" is
   Still opening oysters at the door.
Is Terrè still alive and able?
   I recollect his droll grimace;
He'd come and smile before your table
   And hope you liked your Bouillabaisse.

We enter—nothing's changed or older.
   "How's Monsieur Terrè, waiter, pray?"
The waiter stares and shrugs his shoulder—
   "Monsieur is dead this many a day."
"It is the lot of saint and sinner,
   So honest Terrè's run his race."
"What will Monsieur require for dinner?"
   "Say, do you still cook Bouillabaisse?"

"Oh, oui, Monsieur," is the waiter's answer,
   "Quel vin, Monsieur, désire-t-il?"
"Tell me a good one." "That I can, sir:
   The Chambertin with yellow seal."
"So Terrè's gone," I say, and sink in
   My old accustom'd corner place;
"He's done with feasting and with drinking,
   With Burgundy and Bouillabaisse."

My old accustom'd corner here is,
   The table still is in the nook;
Ah! vanish'd many a busy year is;
   This well-known chair since last I took,
When first I saw ye, "cari luoghi,"
   I'd scarce a beard upon my face,
And now a grizzled, grim old fogy,
   I sit and wait for Bouillabaisse.

Where are you, old companions trusty
   Of early days met here to dine?
Come, waiter! quick, a flagon crusty,
   I'll pledge them in the good old wine.
The kind old voices and old faces
   My memory can quick retrace;
Around the board they take their places,
   And share the wine and Bouillabaisse.

There's Jack has made a wondrous marriage,
   There's laughing Tom is laughing yet,
There's brave Augustus drives his carriage,
   There's poor old Fred in the "Gazette";
On James's head the grass is growing:
   Good Lord! the world has wagged a-pace,
Since here we set the claret flowing
   And drank, and ate the Bouillabaisse.

Ah me! how quick the days are flitting,
   I mind me of the time that's gone,
When here I'd sit, as now I'm sitting
   In this same place—but not alone.
A fair young form was nestled near me,
   A dear, dear face looked fondly up,
And sweetly spoke, and smiled to cheer me—
   There's no one now to share my cup.

I drink it as the Fates ordain it.
   Come, fill it, and have done with rhymes:
Fill up the lonely glass and drain it
   In memory of dear old times.
Welcome the wine, whate'er the seal is,
   And sit you down and say your grace
With thankful heart whate'er the meat is.
   —Here comes the smoking Bouillabaisse!

THE AGE OF WISDOM

Ho, pretty page, with the dimpled chin,
  That never has known the barber's shear,
All your wish is woman to win,
This is the way that boys begin,—
  Wait till you come to Forty Year.

Curly gold locks cover foolish brains,
  Billing and cooing is all your cheer;
Sighing and singing of midnight strains,
Under Bonnybell's window panes,—
  Wait till you come to Forty Year.

Forty times over let Michaelmas pass,
  Grizzling hair the brain doth clear—
Then you know a boy is an ass,
Then you know the worth of a lass,
  Once you have come to Forty Year.

Pledge me round, I bid ye declare,
  All good fellows whose beards are grey,
Did not the fairest of the fair
Common grow and wearisome ere
  Fver a month was passed away?

The reddest lips that ever have kissed,
  The brightest eyes that ever have shone,
May pray and whisper and we not list,
Or look away, and never be missed,
  Ere yet ever a month is gone.

Gillian's dead, God rest her bier,
  How I loved her twenty years syne!
Marian's married, but I sit here
Alone and merry at Forty Year,
  Dipping my nose in the Gascon wine.

Edward Lear

THE AKOND OF SWAT

Who, or why, or which, or *what,*   Is the Akond of Swat

Is he tall or short, or dark or fair?
Does he sit on a stool or a sofa or
    chair,   or SQUAT?
                    The Akond of Swat?

Is he wise or foolish, young or old?
Does he drink his soup and his coffee
    cold,   or HOT,
                    The Akond of Swat

Does he sing or whistle, jabber or talk,
And when riding abroad does he
    gallop or walk,   or TROT,
                    The Akond of Swat

Does he wear a turban, a fez, or a hat?
Does he sleep on a mattress, a bed, or
    a mat,   or a COT,
                    The Akond of Swat

When he writes a copy in round-hand
    size,
Does he cross his T's and finish his
    I's   with a DOT,
                    The Akond of Swat

Can he write a letter concisely clear
Without a speck or a smudge or
    smear   or BLOT,
                    The Akond of Swat

Do his people like him extremely
    well?
Or do they, whenever they can, rebel,   or PLOT,
            The Akond of Swat?

If he catches them then, either old or
    young,
Does he have them chopped in pieces
    or hung,   or *shot*,
            The Akond of Swat?

Do his people prig in the lanes or
    park?
Or even at times, when days are dark,   GARROTE?
            O the Akond of Swat?

Does he study the wants of his own
    dominion?
Or doesn't he care for public opinion   a JOT,
            The Akond of Swat?

To amuse his mind do his people
    show him
Pictures, or any one's last new poem,   or WHAT,
            For the Akond of Swat?

At night if he suddenly screams and
    wakes,
Do they bring him only a few small
    cakes,   or a LOT,
            For the Akond of Swat?

Does he live on turnips, tea, or tripe?
Does he like his shawl to be marked
    with a stripe,   or a DOT,
            The Akond of Swat?

Does he like to lie on his back in a
    boat
Like the lady who lived in that isle
    remote,   SHALLOTT,
                                     The Akond of Swat?

Is he quiet, or always making a fuss?
Is his steward a Swiss or a Swede or
    a Russ,   or a SCOT,
                                     The Akond of Swat?

Does he like to sit by the calm blue
    wave?
Or to sleep and snore in a dark green
    cave,   or a GROTT,
                                     The Akond of Swat?

Does he drink small beer from a silver
    jug?
Or a bowl? or a glass? or a cup? or
    a mug?   or a POT,
                                     The Akond of Swat?

Does he beat his wife with a gold-
    topped pipe,
When she lets the gooseberries grow
    too ripe,   or ROT,
                                     The Akond of Swat?

Does he wear a white tie when he
    dines with friends,
And tie it neat in a bow with ends,   or a KNOT,
                                     The Akond of Swat?

Does he like new cream, and hate
    mince-pies?
When he looks at the sun does he
    wink his eyes,   or NOT,
                                     The Akond of Swat?

Does he teach his subjects to roast
    and bake?
Does he sail about on an inland lake,   in a YACHT,
                               The Akond of Swat?

Some one, or nobody, knows I wot
Who or which or why or what   Is the Akond of Swat!

*

THE NUTCRACKERS AND THE SUGAR-TONGS

I

The Nutcrackers sate by a plate on the table;
  The Sugar-tongs sate by a plate at his side;
And the Nutcrackers said, "Don't you wish we were able
  Along the blue hills and green meadows to ride?
Must we drag on this stupid existence forever,
  So idle and weary, so full of remorse,
While every one else takes his pleasure, and never
  Seems happy unless he is riding a horse?

II

"Don't you think we could ride without being instructed,
  Without any saddle or bridle or spur?
Our legs are so long, and so aptly constructed,
  I'm sure that an accident could not occur.
Let us all of a sudden hop down from the table,
  And hustle downstairs, and each jump on a horse!
Shall we try? Shall we go? Do you think we are able?"
  The Sugar-tongs answered distinctly, "Of course!"

III

So down the long staircase they hopped in a minute;
  The Sugar-tongs snapped, and the Crackers said "Crack!"
The stable was open; the horses were in it:
  Each took out a pony, and jumped on his back.

The Cat in a fright scrambled out of the doorway;
  The Mice tumbled out of a bundle of hay;
The brown and white Rats, and the black ones from Norway,
  Screamed out, "They are taking the horses away!"

IV

The whole of the household was filled with amazement:
The Cups and the Saucers danced madly about;
The Plates and the Dishes looked out of the casement;
  The Salt-cellar stood on his head with a shout;
The Spoons, with a clatter, looked out of the lattice;
  The Mustard-pot climbed up the gooseberry-pies;
The Soup-ladle peeped through a heap of veal-patties,
  And squeaked with a ladle-like scream of surprise.

V

The Frying-pan said, "It's an awful delusion!"
  The Tea-kettle hissed, and grew black in the face;
And they all rushed downstairs in the wildest confusion
  To see the great Nutcracker-Sugar-tong race.
And out of the stable, with screamings and laughter
  (Their ponies were cream-coloured, speckled with brown),
The Nutcrackers first, and the Sugar-tongs after,
  Rode all round the yard, and then all round the town.

VI

They rode through the street, and they rode by the station;
  They galloped away to the beautiful shore;
In silence they rode, and "made no observation,"
  Save this: "We will never go back any more!"
And still you might hear, till they rode out of hearing,
  The Sugar-tongs snap, and the Crackers say "Crack!"
Till, far in the distance their forms disappearing,
  They faded away; and they never came back!

Arthur Hugh Clough

FROM *SPECTATOR AB EXTRA*

As I sat at the café I said to myself,
They may talk as they please about what they call pelf,
They may sneer as they like about eating and drinking,
But help it I cannot, I cannot help thinking
  How pleasant it is to have money, heigh-ho!
  How pleasant it is to have money....

They may talk as they please about what they call pelf,
And how one ought never to think of one's-self,
How pleasures of thought surpass eating and drinking,
My pleasure of thought is the pleasure of thinking
  How pleasant it is to have money, heigh-ho!
  How pleasant it is to have money....

Charles Kingsley

SING HEIGH-HO!

There sits a bird on every tree
  Sing heigh-ho!
There sits a bird on every tree,
And courts his love, as I do thee;
  Sing heigh-ho, and heigh-ho!
Young maids must marry.

There grows a flower on every bough,
  Sing heigh-ho!
There grows a flower on every bough,
Its petals kiss—I'll show you how:
  Sing heigh-ho, and heigh-ho!
Young maids must marry.

From sea to stream the salmon roam:
   Sing heigh-ho!
From sea to stream the salmon roam:
Each finds a mate, and leads her home;
   Sing heigh-ho, and heigh-ho!
Young maids must marry.

The sun's a bridegroom, earth a bride,
   Sing heigh-ho!
They court from morn till eventide:
The earth shall pass, but love abide;
   Sing heigh-ho, and heigh-ho!
Young maids must marry.

Frederick Locker-Lampson

TO MY GRANDMOTHER

Suggested by a picture by Mr. Romney

This Relative of mine,
Was she seventy-and-nine
   When she died?
By the canvas may be seen
How she look'd at seventeen,
   As a bride.

Beneath a summer tree
Her maiden reverie
   Has a charm;
Her ringlets are in taste;
What an arm! and what a waist
   For an arm!

With her bridal-wreath, bouquet,
Lace farthingale, and gay
   Falbala,
If Romney's touch be true,
What a lucky dog were you,
   Grandpapa!

Her lips are sweet as love;
They are parting! Do they move?
   Are they dumb?
Her eyes are blue, and beam
Beseechingly, and seem
   To say, "Come!"

What funny fancy slips
From atween these cherry lips?
   Whisper me,
Fair Sorceress in paint,
What canon says I mayn't
   Marry thee?

That good-for-nothing Time
Has a confidence sublime!
   When I first
Saw this Lady, in my youth,
Her winters had, forsooth
   Done their worst.

Her locks, as white as snow,
Once shamed the swarthy crow;
   By-and-by
That fowl's avenging sprite
Set his cruel foot for spite
   Near her eye.

Her rounded form was lean,
And her silk was bombazine;
    Well I wot
With her needles would she sit,
And for hours would she knit,—
    Would she not?

Ah perishable clay!
Her charms had dropt away
    One by one;
But if she heaved a sigh
With a burthen, it was, "Thy
    Will be done."

In travail, as in tears,
With the fardel of her years
    Overprest,
In mercy she was borne
Where the weary and the worn
    Are at rest.

Oh, if you now are there,
And sweet as once you were,
    Grandmamma,
This nether world agrees
You'll all the better please
    Grandpapa.

*

A TERRIBLE INFANT

I recollect a nurse call'd Ann,
  Who carried me about the grass,
And one fine day a fine young man
  Came up, and kiss'd the pretty Lass:

She did not make the least objection!
                    Thinks I, "Aha!
When I can talk I'll tell Mamma."
—*And that's my earliest recollection.*

*

ROTTEN ROW

I hope I'm fond of much that's good,
    As well as much that's gay;
I'd like the country if I could;
    I love the Park in May;
And when I ride in Rotten Row,
I wonder why they call'd it so.

A lively scene on turf and road;
    The crowd is bravely drest:
The *Ladies' Mile* has overflow'd,
    The chairs are in request:
The nimble air, so soft, so clear,
Can hardly stir a ringlet here.

I'll halt beneath those pleasant trees,—
    And drop my bridle-rein,
And, quite alone, indulge at ease
    The philosophic vein:
I'll moralize on all I see—
Yes, it was all arranged for me!

Forsooth, and on a livelier Spot
    The sunbeam never shines.
Fair ladies here can talk and trot
    With statesmen and divines:
Could I have chosen, I've have been
A Duke, a Beauty, or a Dean.

What grooms! What gallant gentlemen!
    What well-appointed hacks!
What glory in their pace, and then
    What beauty on their backs!
My Pegasus would never flag
If weighted as my Lady's nag.

But where is now the courtly troop
    That once rode laughing by?
I miss the curls of Cantilupe,
    The laugh of Lady Di:
They all could laugh from night to morn,
And Time has laugh'd them all to scorn.

I then could frolic in the van
    With dukes and dandy earls;
Then I was thought a *nice* young man
    By rather *nice* young girls!
I've half a mind to join Miss Browne,
And try one canter up and down.

Ah, no—I'll linger here awhile,
    And dream of days of yore;
For me bright eyes have lost the smile,
    The sunny smile they wore:—
Perhaps they say what I'll allow,
That I'm not quite so handsome now.

*

LOULOU AND HER CAT

Good pastry is vended
    In Cité Fadette;
Maison Pons can make splendid
    Brioche and *galette*.

M'sieu Pons is so fat that
  He's laid on the shelf;
Madame had a Cat that
  Was fat as herself.

Long hair, soft as satin,
  A musical purr,
'Gainst the window she'd flatten
  Her delicate fur.

I drove Lou to see what
  Our neighbours were at,
In rapture, cried she, "What
  An exquisite cat!

"What whiskers! She's purring
  All over. Regale
Our eyes, *Puss,* by stirring
  Thy feathery tail!

"*M'sieu Pons,* will you sell her?"
  "*Ma femme est sortie,*
Your offer I'll tell her;
  But will she?" says he.

Yet *Pons* was persuaded
  To part with the prize:
(Our bargain was aided,
  My Lou, by your eyes!)

From his *légitime* save him,—
  My spouse I prefer,
For I warrant *his* gave him
  Un mauvais quart d'heure.

I am giving a pleasant
    Grimalkin to Lou,
—Ah, *Puss,* what a present
    I'm giving to you!

*

OUR PHOTOGRAPHS

She play'd me false, but that's not why
I haven't quite forgiven Di,
        Although I've tried:
This curl was hers, so brown, so bright,
She gave it me one blissful night,
        And—more beside!

Our photographs were group'd together;
She wore the darling hat and feather
        That I adore;
In profile by her side I sat
Reading my poetry—but that
        She'd heard before.

Why, after all, Di threw me over
I never knew, I can't discover,
        And hardly guess;
May be Smith's lyrics she decided
Were sweeter than the sweetest I did—
        I acquiesce.

A week before their wedding day,
That Beast was call'd in haste away
        To join the Staff.
Di gave him then, with tearful mien,
Her only photograph. I've seen
        That photograph,

I've seen it in Smith's pocket-book!
Just think! her hat, her tender look,
  Are now that Brute's!
Before she gave it, off she cut
My body, head, and lyrics, but
She was obliged, the little Slut,
  To leave my Boots.

Coventry Patmore

THE KISS

'I saw you take his kiss!' ' 'Tis true.'
 'O modesty!' ' 'Twas strictly kept:
He thought me asleep—at least, I knew
 He thought I thought he thought I slept.'

Mortimer Collins

MARTIAL IN LONDON

Exquisite wines and comestibles,
 From Slater, and Fortnum and Mason;
Billiard, écarté, and chess tables;
 Water in vast marble basin;
Luminous books (not voluminous)
To read under beech-trees cacuminous;
One friend, who is fond of a distich,
And doesn't get too syllogistic;
A valet, who knows of the complete art
Of service—a maiden, his sweetheart:
Give me these, in some rural pavilion,
And I'll envy no Rothschild his million.

Dante Gabriel Rossetti

THE BALLAD OF DEAD LADIES

Tell me now in what hidden way is
  Lady Flora the lovely Roman?
Where's Hipparchia, and where is Thaïs,
  Neither of them the fairer woman?
  Where is Echo, beheld of no man,
Only heard on river and mere,—
  She whose beauty was more than human? ...
But where are the snows of yester-year?

Where's Héloise, the learned nun,
  For whose sake Abeillard, I ween,
Lost manhood and put priesthood on?
  (From Love he won such dule and teen!)
  And where, I pray you, is the Queen
Who willed that Buridan should steer
  Sewed in a sack's mouth down the Seine? ...
But where are the snows of yester-year?

White Queen Blanche, like a queen of lilies,
  With a voice like any mermaiden,—
Bertha Broadfoot, Beatrice, Alice,
  And Ermengarde the Lady of Maine,—
  And that good Joan whom Englishmen
At Rouen doomed and burned her there,—
  Mother of God, where are they then? ...
But where are the snows of yester-year?

Nay, never ask this week, fair lord,
  Where they are gone, nor yet this year,
Except with this for an overword,—
  "But where are the snows of yester-year?"
                    Translated from François Villon

Major Robert C. MacGregor

WITH TWO FAIR GIRLS

With two fair girls—dark night above—was I,
Caressing one, carest the other by:
While, greedily, Rose drew me to her kiss,
More rare with Susan was my stolen bliss;
Careful to cheat—lest lips too loud betray'd—
The jealous anger of each neighbour maid.
Inly I groan'd: To love, and lov'd to be,
Alas! alike is punishment to me.

Translated from the Greek Anthology

Charles S. Calverley

LINES SUGGESTED BY THE FOURTEENTH OF FEBRUARY

Darkness succeeds to twilight:
Through lattice and through skylight,
The stars no doubt, if one looked out,
Might be observed to shine:
And sitting by the embers
I elevate my members
On a stray chair, and then and there
Commence a Valentine.

Yea! by St. Valentinus,
Emma shall not be minus
What all young ladies, whate'er their grade is,
Expect to-day no doubt:
Emma the fair, the stately—
Whom I beheld so lately,

Smiling beneath the snow-white wreath
    Which told that she was "out."

Wherefore fly to her, swallow,
    And mention that I'd "follow,"
And "pipe and trill," et cetera, till
    I died, had I but wings:
    Say the North's "true and tender,"
    The South an old offender;
And hint in fact, with your well-known tact,
    All kinds of pretty things.

Say I grow hourly thinner,
    Simply abhor my dinner—
Tho' I do try and absorb some viand
    Each day, for form's sake merely:
    And ask her, when all's ended,
    And I am found extended,
With vest blood-spotted and cut carotid,
    To think on Hers sincerely.

*

"FOREVER"

Forever; 'tis a single word!
    Our rude forefathers deem'd it two:
Can you imagine so absurd
        A view?
Forever! What abysms of woe
    The word reveals, what frenzy, what
Despair! For ever (printed so)
        Did not.

It looks, ah me! how trite and tame!
　　It fails to sadden or appal
Or solace—it is not the same
　　　　At all.

O thou to whom it first occurr'd
　　To solder the disjoin'd, and dower
Thy native language with a word
　　　　Of power:

We bless thee! Whether far or near
　　Thy dwelling, whether dark or fair
Thy kingly brow, is neither here
　　　　Nor there.

But in men's hearts shall be thy throne,
　　While the great pulse of England beats:
Thou coiner of a word unknown
　　　　To Keats!

And nevermore must printer do
　　As men did long ago; but run
"For" into "ever," bidding two
　　　　Be one.

Forever! passion-fraught, it throws
　　O'er the dim page a gloom, a glamour:
It's sweet, it's strange; and I suppose
　　　　It's grammar.

Forever! 'Tis a single word!
　　And yet our fathers deem'd it two:
Nor am I confident they err'd;
　　　　Are you?

ODE TO TOBACCO

Thou who, when fears attack,
Bidst them avaunt, and Black
Care, at the horseman's back
        Perching, unseatest;
Sweet, when the morn is gray;
Sweet, when they've cleared away
Lunch; and at close of day
        Possibly sweetest:

I have a liking old
For thee, though manifold
Stories, I know, are told,
        Not to thy credit;
How one (or two at most)
Drops make a cat a ghost—
Useless, except to roast—
        Doctors have said it:

How they who use fusees
All grow by slow degrees
Brainless as chimpanzees,
        Meagre as lizards:
Go mad, and beat their wives;
Plunge (after shocking lives)
Razors and carving knives
        Into their gizzards.

Confound such knavish tricks!
Yet know I five or six
Smokers who freely mix
        Still with their neighbours;

Jones—(who, I'm glad to say,
  Asked leave of Mrs. J.)—
Daily absorbs a clay
    After his labours.

Cats may have had their goose
Cooked by tobacco-juice;
Still why deny its use
    Thoughtfully taken?
We're not as tabbies are:
Smith, take a fresh cigar!
Jones; the tobacco-jar!
    Here's to thee, Bacon!

*

CHANGED

I know not why my soul is rack'd:
  Why I ne'er smile as was my wont:
I only know that, as a fact,
    I don't.
I used to roam o'er glen and glade
  Buoyant and blithe as other folk:
And not unfrequently I made
    A joke.

A minstrel's fire within me burn'd.
  I'd sing, as one whose heart must break,
Lay upon lay: I nearly learn'd
    To shake.
All day I sang; of love, of fame,
  Of fights our fathers fought of yore,
Until the thing almost became
    A bore.

I cannot sing the old songs now!
   It is not that I deem them low;
'Tis that I can't remember how
     They go.
I could not range the hills till high
   Above me stood the summer moon:
And as to dancing, I could fly
     As soon.

The sports, to which with boyish glee
   I sprang erewhile, attract no more;
Although I am but sixty-three
     Or four.
Nay, worse than that, I've seem'd of late
   To shrink from happy boyhood--boys
Have grown so noisy, and I hate
     A noise.

They fright me, when the beech is green,
   By swarming up its stem for eggs:
They drive their horrid hoops between
     My legs:--
It's idle to repine, I know;
   I'll tell you what I'll do instead:
I'll drink my arrowroot, and go
     To bed.

*

ON THE BEACH

LINES BY A PRIVATE TUTOR

When the young Augustus Edward
Has reluctantly gone bedward
(He's the urchin I am privileged to teach),

From my left-hand waistcoat pocket
  I extract a batter'd locket
And I commune with it, walking on the beach.

  I had often yearn'd for something
  That would love me, e'en a dumb thing;
But such happiness seem'd always out of reach:
  Little boys are off like arrows
  With their little spades and barrows,
When they see me bearing down upon the beach;

  And although I'm rather handsome,
  Tiny babes, when I would dance 'em
On my arm, set up so horrible a screech
  That I pitch them to their nurses
  With (I fear me) mutter'd curses,
And resume my lucubrations on the beach.

  And the rabbits won't come nigh me,
  And the gulls observe and fly me,
And I doubt, upon my honour, if a leech
  Would stick on me as on others,
  And I know if I had brothers
They would cut me when we met upon the beach.

  So at last I bought this trinket;
  For (although I love to think it)
'Twasn't *given* me, with a pretty little speech:
  No! I bought it of a pedlar, .
  Brown and wizen'd as a medlar,
Who was hawking odds and ends about the beach.

  But I've managed, very nearly,
  To believe that I was dearly
Loved by Somebody, who (blushing like a peach)

Flung it o'er me saying, "Wear it
   For my sake"—and I declare, it
Seldom strikes me that I bought it on the beach.

   I can see myself revealing
   Unsuspected depths of feeling,
As, in tones that half upbraid and half beseech,
   I aver with what delight I
   Would give anything—my right eye—
For a souvenir of our stroll upon the beach.

   O! that eye that never glisten'd
   And that voice to which I've listen'd
But in fancy, how I dote upon them each!
   How regardless what o'clock it
   Is, I pore upon that locket
Which does not contain her portrait, on the beach!

   As if something were inside it
   I laboriously hide it,
And a rather pretty sermon you might preach
   Upon Fantasy, selecting
   For your "instance" the affecting
Tale of me and my proceedings on the beach.

   I depict her, ah, how charming!
   I portray myself alarming
Her by swearing I would "mount the deadly breach."
   Or engage in any scrimmage
   For a glimpse of her sweet image,
Or her shadow, or her footprint on the beach.

   And I'm ever, ever seeing
   My imaginary Being,
And I'd rather that my marrowbones should bleach

In the winds, than that a cruel
Fate should snatch from me the jewel
Which I bought for one and sixpence on the beach.

*

CONTENTMENT

AFTER THE MANNER OF HORACE

Friend, there be they on whom mishap
    Or never or so rarely comes,
That, when they think thereof, they snap
      Derisive thumbs:

And there be they who lightly lose
    Their all, yet feel no aching void;
Should aught annoy them, they refuse
      To be annoy'd:

And fain would I be e'en as these!
    Life is with such all beer and skittles;
They are not difficult to please
      About their victuals:

The trout, the grouse, the early pea,
    By such, if there, are freely taken;
If not, they munch with equal glee
      Their bit of bacon:

And when they wax a little gay
    And chaff the public after luncheon,
If they're confronted with a stray
      Policeman's truncheon,

They gaze thereat with outstretch'd necks,
    And laughter which no threats can smother,
And tell the horror-stricken X
      That he's another.

In snowtime if they cross a spot
　　Where unsuspected boys have slid,
They fall not down—though they would not
　　　　Mind if they did:

When the spring rosebud which they wear
　　Breaks short and tumbles from its stem,
No thought of being angry e'er
　　　　Dawns upon them;

Though 'twas Jemima's hand that placed,
　　(As well you ween) at evening's hour,
In the loved button-hole that chaste
　　　　And cherish'd flower.

And when they travel, if they find
　　That they have left their pocket-compass
Or Murray or thick boots behind,
　　　　They raise no rumpus,

But plod serenely on without:
　　Knowing it's better to endure
The evil which beyond all doubt
　　　　You cannot cure.

When for that early train they're late,
　　They do not make their woes the text
Of sermons in the Times, but wait
　　　　On for the next;

And jump inside, and only grin
　　Should it appear that that dry wag,
The guard, omitted to put in
　　　　Their carpet-bag.

LOVE

Canst thou love me, lady?
  I've not learn'd to woo;
Thou art on the shady
  Side of sixty, too.
Still I love thee dearly!
  Thou hast lands and pelf:
But I love thee merely
  Merely for thyself.

Wilt thou love me, fairest?
  Though thou art not fair;
And I think thou wearest
  Someone-else's hair.
Thou could'st love, though, dearly;
  And, as I am told,
Thou art very nearly
  Worth thy weight in gold.

Dost thou love me, sweet one?
  Tell me that thou dost!
Women fairly beat one
  But I think thou must.
Thou art loved so dearly:
  I am plain, but then
Thou (to speak sincerely)
  Art as plain again.

Love me, bashful fairy!
  I've an empty purse:
And I've "moods," which vary;
  Mostly for the worst.
Still, I love thee dearly:
  Though I make (I feel)

Love a little queerly,
    I'm as true as steel.

Love me, swear to love me
    (As you know, they do)
By yon heaven above me
    And its changeless blue.
Love me, lady, dearly,
    If you'll be so good;
Though I don't see clearly
    On what ground you should.

Love me—ah! or love me
    Not, but be my bride!
Do not simply shove me
    (So to speak) aside!
P'raps it would be dearly
    Purchased at the price;
But a hundred yearly
    Would be very nice.

Lewis Carroll

JABBERWOCKY

'Twas brillig, and the slithy toves
    Did gyre and gimble in the wabe;
All mimsy were the borogroves,
    And the mome raths outgrabe.

"Beware the Jabberwock, my son!
    The jaws that bite, the claws that catch!
Beware the Jubjub bird, and shun
    The frumious Bandersnatch!"

He took his vorpal sword in hand:
  Long time the manxome foe he sought—
So rested he by the tum-tum tree,
  And stood awhile in thought.

And as in uffish thought he stood,
  The Jabberwock, with eyes of flame,
Came whiffling through the tulgey wood,
  And burbled as it came!

One, two! One, two! And through and through
  The vorpal blade went snicker-snack!
He left it dead, and with its head
  He went galumphing back.

"And hast thou slain the Jabberwock?
  Come to my arms, my beamish boy!
O frabjous day! Callooh! Callay!"
  He chortled in his joy.

'Twas brillig, and the slithy toves
  Did gyre and gimble in the wabe;
All mimsy were the borogroves,
  And the mome raths outgrabe.

*

SHE'S ALL MY FANCY PAINTED HIM

  She's all my fancy painted him,
    (I make no idle boast);
  If he or you had lost a limb,
    Which would have suffered most?

  He said that you had been to her,
    And seen me here before:
  But, in another character
    She was the same of yore.

There was not one that spoke to us,
    Of all that thronged the street;
So he sadly got into a 'bus,
    And pattered with his feet.

They told me you had been to her,
    And mentioned me to him;
She gave me a good character,
    But said I could not swim.

He sent them word I had not gone
    (We know it to be true);
If she should push the matter on,
    What would become of you?

I gave her one, they gave him two,
    You gave us three or more;
They all returned from him to you,
    Though they were mine before.

If I or she should chance to be
    Involved in this affair,
He trusts to you to set them free,
    Exactly as we were.

My notion was that you had been
    (Before she had this fit)
An obstacle that came between
    Him, and ourselves, and it.

Don't let him know she like them best,
    For this must ever be
A secret, kept from all the rest,
    Between yourself and me.

Charles Henry Webb

DICTUM SAPIENTI

That 'tis well to be off with the old love
   Before one is on with the new
Has somehow passed into a proverb,—
   But I never have found it true.

No love can be quite like the old love;
   Whate'er may be said for the new—
And if you dismiss me, my darling,
   You may come to this thinking, too.

Were the proverb not wiser if mended,
   And the fickle and wavering told
To be sure they're on with the new love
   Before they are off with the old?

Sir W. S. Gilbert

THE FAMILY FOOL

Oh! a private buffoon is a light-hearted loon,
   If you listen to popular rumour;
From morning to night he's so joyous and bright,
   And he bubbles with wit and good humour!
He's so quaint and so terse, both in prose and in verse;
   Yet though people forgive his transgression,
There are one or two rules that all Family Fools
   Must observe if they love their profession.
     There are one or two rules,
      Half-a-dozen, maybe,
     That all family fools,
      Of whatever degree,
Must observe if they love their profession.

If you wish to succeed as a jester, you'll need
    To consider each person's auricular;
What is all right for B. would quite scandalize C.
    (For C. is so very particular);
And D. may be dull, and E.'s very thick skull
    Is as empty of brains as a ladle;
While F. is F sharp, and will cry with a carp,
    That he's known your best joke from his cradle!
        When your humour they flout,
           You can't let yourself go;
        And it *does* put you out
           When a person says, "Oh!
I have known that old joke from my cradle!"

If your master is surly, from getting up early
    (And tempers are short in the morning),
An inopportune joke is enough to provoke
    Him to give you, at once, a month's warning.
Then if you refrain, he is at you again,
    For he likes to get value for money,
He'll ask then and there, with an insolent stare,
    "If you know that you're paid to be funny?"
        It adds to the tasks
           Of a merryman's place,
        When your principal asks,
           With a scowl on his face,
If you know that you're paid to be funny?

Comes a Bishop, maybe, or a solemn D.D.—
    Oh! beware of his anger provoking
Better not pull his hair—don't stick pins in his chair;
    He won't understand practical joking.
If the jests that you crack have an orthodox smack,
    You may get a bland smile from these sages;

But should it, by chance, be imported from France,
  Half-a-crown is stopped out of your wages!
    It's a general rule,
      Though your zeal it may quench
    If the Family Fool
      Makes a joke that's *too* French,
  Half-a-crown is stopped out of his wages!

Though your head it may rack with a bilious attack,
  And your senses with toothache you're losing,
Don't be mopy and flat—they don't fine you for that
  If you're properly quaint and amusing!
Though your wife ran away with a soldier that day
  And took with her your trifle of money;
Bless your heart, they don't mind—they're exceedingly
    kind—
  They don't blame you—as long as you're funny!
    It's a comfort to feel
      If your partner should flit,
    Though *you* suffer a deal,
      They don't mind it a bit—
  They don't blame you—so long as you're funny!

*

KING GOODHEART

There lived a king, as I've been told
In the wonder-working days of old,
When hearts were twice as good as gold,
    And twenty times as mellow.
Good temper triumphed in his face,
And in his heart he found a place
For all the erring human race
    And every wretched fellow.

When he had Rhenish wine to drink
It made him very sad to think
That some, at junket or at jink,
    Must be content with toddy:
He wished all men as rich as he
(And he was rich as rich could be),
So to the top of every tree
    Promoted everybody.

Ambassadors cropped up like hay,
Prime Ministers and such as they
Grew like asparagus in May,
    And Dukes were three a penny:
Lord Chancellors were cheap as sprats,
And Bishops in their shovel hats
Were plentiful as tabby cats—
    If possible, too many.

On every side Field-Marshals gleamed,
Small beer were Lords-Lieutenants deemed,
With Admirals the ocean teemed,
    All round his wide dominions;
And Party Leaders you might meet
In twos and threes in every street
Maintaining, with no little heat,
    Their various opinions.

That King, although no one denies,
His heart was of abnormal size,
Yet he'd have acted otherwise
    If he had been acuter.
The end is easily foretold,
When every blessed thing you hold
Is made of silver, or of gold,
    You long for simple pewter.

When you have nothing else to wear
But cloth of gold and satins rare,
For cloth of gold you cease to care—
  Up goes the price of shoddy:
In short, whoever you may be,
To this conclusion you'll agree,
When every one is somebody,
  Then no one's anybody!

   *

THE DUKE OF PLAZA-TORO

In enterprise of martial kind,
  When there was any fighting,
He led his regiment from behind
  (He found it less exciting).
But when away his regiment ran,
  His place was at the fore, O—
   That celebrated,
   Cultivated,
   Underrated
    Nobleman,
  The Duke of Plaza-Toro!
In the first and foremost flight, ha, ha!
You always found that knight, ha, ha!
   That celebrated,
   Cultivated,
   Underrated
    Nobleman,
  The Duke of Plaza-Toro!

When, to evade Destruction's hand,
  To hide they all proceeded,
No soldier in that gallant band
  Hid half as well as he did.

He lay concealed throughout the war,
  And so preserved his gore, O!
    That unaffected,
    Undetected,
    Well connected
     Warrior,
  The Duke of Plaza-Toro!
In every doughty deed, ha, ha!
He always took the lead, ha, ha!
    That unaffected,
    Undetected,
    Well connected
     Warrior,
  The Duke of Plaza-Toro!

When told that they would all be shot
  Unless they left the service,
That hero hesitated not,
  So marvellous his nerve is.
He sent his resignation in,
  The first of all his corps, O!
    That very knowing,
    Overflowing,
    Easy-going
     Paladin,
  The Duke of Plaza-Toro!
To men of grosser clay, ha, ha!
He always showed the way, ha, ha!
    That very knowing,
    Overflowing,
    Easy-going
     Paladin,
  The Duke of Plaza-Toro!

OUT OF SORTS

When you find you're a broken-down critter,
Who is all of a trimmle and twitter,
With your palate unpleasantly bitter,
    As if you'd just bitten a pill—
When your legs are as thin as dividers,
And you're plagued with unruly insiders,
And your spine is all creepy with spiders,
    And you're highly gamboge in the gill—
When you've got a beehive in your head,
    And a sewing machine in each ear,
And you feel that you've eaten your bed,
    And you've got a bad headache *down here*—
      When such facts are about,
        And these symptoms you find
          In your body or crown—
      Well, it's time to look out,
        You may make up your mind
        You had better lie down!

When your lips are all smeary—like tallow,
And your tongue is decidedly yallow,
With a pint of warm oil in your swallow,
    And a pound of tin-tacks in your chest—
When you're down in the mouth with the vapours,
And all over your new Morris papers
Black-beetles are cutting their capers,
    And crawly things never at rest—
When you doubt if your head is your own,
    And you jump when an open door slams—
Then you've got to a state which is known
    To the medical world as "jim-jams."

If such symptoms you find
    In your body or head,
        They're not easy to quell—
You may make up your mind
    You are better in bed,
        For you're not at all well!

*

THE HUMANE MIKADO

A more humane Mikado never
    Did in Japan exist;
        To nobody second,
        I'm certainly reckoned
    A true philanthropist.
It is my very humane endeavour
    To make, to some extent,
        Each evil liver
        A running river
    Of harmless merriment.

    My object all sublime
    I shall achieve in time—
    To let the punishment fit the crime—
        The punishment fit the crime;
    And make each prisoner pent
    Unwillingly represent
    A source of innocent merriment—
        Of innocent merriment!

All prosy dull society sinners,
    Who chatter and bleat and bore,
        Are sent to hear sermons

From mystical Germans
Who preach from ten to four:
The amateur tenor, whose vocal villainies
    All desire to shirk,
        Shall, during off-hours,
        Exhibit his powers
    To Madame Tussaud's waxwork:
The lady who dyes a chemical yellow,
    Or stains her grey hair puce,
        Or pinches her figger,
        Is blacked like a nigger
    With permanent walnut juice:
The idiot who, in railway carriages,
    Scribbles on window panes,
        We only suffer
        To ride on a buffer
    In Parliamentary trains.

        My object all sublime
        I shall achieve in time—
    To let the punishment fit the crime—
        The punishment fit the crime;
        And make each prisoner pent
        Unwillingly represent
    A source of innocent merriment—
        Of innocent merriment!

The advertising quack who wearies
    With tales of countless cures,
        His teeth, I've enacted,
        Shall all be extracted
    By terrified amateurs:

The music-hall singer attends a series
  Of masses and fugues and "ops"
     By Bach, interwoven
     With Spohr and Beethoven,
      At classical Monday Pops:
The billiard sharp whom any one catches
  His doom's extremely hard—
     He's made to dwell
     In a dungeon cell
  On a spot that's always barred;
And there he plays extravagant matches
  In fitless finger-stalls,
     On a cloth untrue
     With a twisted cue,
  And elliptical billiard balls!

     My object all sublime
     I shall achieve in time—
  To let the punishment fit the crime—
      The punishment fit the crime;
     And make each prisoner pent
     Unwillingly represent
  A source of innocent merriment,
      Of innocent merriment!

*

THE DISAGREEABLE MAN

If you give me your attention, I will tell you what I am:
I'm a genuine philanthropist—all other kinds are sham.
Each little fault of temper and each social defect
In my erring fellow-creatures, I endeavour to correct.

To all their little weaknesses I open people's eyes,
And little plans to snub the self-sufficient I devise;
I love my fellow-creatures—I do all the good I can—
Yet everybody says I'm such a disagreeable man!
    And I can't think why!

To compliments inflated I've a withering reply,
And vanity I always do my best to mortify;
A charitable action I can skillfully dissect;
And interested motives I'm delighted to detect.
I know everybody's income and what everybody earns,
And I carefully compare it with the income-tax returns;
But to benefit humanity, however much I plan,
Yet everybody says I'm such a disagreeable man!
    And I can't think why!

I'm sure I'm no ascetic; I'm as pleasant as can be;
You'll always find me ready with a crushing repartee;
I've an irritating chuckle, I've a celebrated sneer,
I've an entertaining snigger, I've a fascinating leer;
To everybody's prejudice I know a thing or two;
I can tell a woman's age in half a minute—and I do—
But although I try to make myself as pleasant as I can,
Yet everybody says I'm such a disagreeable man!
    And I can't think why!

*

THE ROVER'S APOLOGY

Oh, gentlemen, listen, I pray;
    Though I own that my heart has been ranging,
Of nature the laws I obey,
    For nature is constantly changing.

The moon in her phases is found,
  The time and the wind and the weather,
The months in succession come round,
  And you don't find two Mondays together.
    Consider the moral, I pray,
      Nor bring a young fellow to sorrow,
    Who loves this young lady to-day,
      And loves that young lady to-morrow!

You cannot eat breakfast all day.
  Nor is it the act of a sinner,
When breakfast is taken away,
  To turn your attention to dinner;
And it's not in the range of belief
  That you could hold him as a glutton,
Who, when he is tired of beef,
  Determines to tackle the mutton.
    But this I am ready to say,
      If it will diminish their sorrow,
    I'll marry this lady to-day,
      And I'll marry that lady to-morrow!

*

THE SUICIDE'S GRAVE

On a tree by a river a little tomtit
      Sang "Willow, titwillow, titwillow!"
And I said to him, "Dicky-bird, why do you sit
      Singing 'Willow, titwillow, titwillow'?
Is it weakness of intellect, birdie?" I cried,
"Or a rather tough worm in your little inside?"
With a shake of his poor little head he replied,
      "Oh, willow, titwillow, titwillow!"

He slapped at his chest, as he sat on that bough,
      Singing "Willow, titwillow, titwillow!"
And a cold perspiration bespangled his brow,
      Oh, willow, titwillow, titwillow!
He sobbed and he sighed, and a gurgle he gave,
Then he threw himself into the billowy wave,
And an echo arose from the suicide's grave—
      "Oh, willow, titwillow, titwillow!"

Now I feel just as sure as I'm sure that my name
      Isn't Willow, titwillow, titwillow,
That 'twas blighted affection that made him exclaim,
      "Oh, willow, titwillow, titwillow!"
And if you remain callous and obdurate, I
Shall perish as he did, and you will know why,
Though I probably shall not exclaim as I die,
      "Oh, willow, titwillow, titwillow!"

*

THE CONTEMPLATIVE SENTRY

When all night long a chap remains
  On sentry-go, to chase monotony
He exercises of his brains,
  That is, assuming that he's got any.
Though never nurtured in the lap
  Of luxury, yet I admonish you,
I am an intellectual chap,
  And think of things that would astonish you.
    I often think it's comical
      How Nature always does contrive
    That every boy and every gal,

That's born into the world alive,
   Is either a little Liberal,
      Or else a little Conservative!
         Fal lal la!

When in that house M.P.'s divide,
   If they've a brain and cerebellum, too,
They've got to leave that brain outside,
   And vote just as their leaders tell 'em to.
But then the prospect of a lot
   Of statesmen, all in close proximity,
A-thinking for themselves, is what
   No man can face with equanimity.
      Then let's rejoice with loud Fal lal
         That Nature wisely does contrive
      That every boy and every gal,
         That's born into the world alive,
      Is either a little Liberal,
         Or else a little Conservative!
            Fal lal la!

*

THE SUSCEPTIBLE CHANCELLOR

The law is the true embodiment
Of everything that's excellent.
It has no kind of fault or flaw,
And I, my lords, embody the Law.
The constitutional guardian I
Of pretty young Wards in Chancery,
All very agreeable girls—and none
Is over the age of twenty-one.
   A pleasant occupation for
   A rather susceptible Chancellor!

But though the compliment implied
Inflates me with legitimate pride,
It nevertheless can't be denied
That it has its inconvenient side.
For I'm not so old, and not so plain,
And I'm quite prepared to marry again,
But there'd be the deuce to pay in the Lords
If I fell in love with one of my Wards:
    Which rather tries my temper, for
    I'm *such* a susceptible Chancellor!

And every one who'd marry a Ward
Must come to me for my accord:
So in my court I sit all day,
Giving agreeable girls away,
With one for him—and one for he—
And one for you—and one for ye—
And one for thou—and one for thee—
But never, oh never a one for me!
    Which is exasperating, for
    A highly susceptible Chancellor!

*

THE ÆSTHETE

If you're anxious for to shine in the high æsthetic line, as
    a man of culture rare,
You must get up all the germs of the transcendental terms,
    and plant them everywhere.
You must lie upon the daisies and discourse in novel phrases
    of your complicated state of mind
(The meaning doesn't matter if it's only idle chatter of a
    transcendental kind).

> And every one will say,
> As you walk your mystic way,
"If this young man expresses himself in terms too deep for
    me,
Why, what a very singularly deep young man this deep
    young man must be!"

Be eloquent in praise of the very dull old days which have
    long since passed away,
And convince 'em, if you can, that the reign of good
    QUEEN ANNE was Culture's palmiest day.
Of course you will pooh-pooh whatever's fresh and new,
    and declare it's crude and mean,
And that Art stopped short in the cultivated court of the
    EMPRESS JOSEPHINE.

> And every one will say,
> As you walk your mystic way,
"If that's not good enough for him which is good enough
    for *me*,
Why, what a very cultivated kind of youth this kind of
    youth must be!"

Then a sentimental passion of a vegetable fashion must
    excite your languid spleen,
An attachment *à la* Plato for a bashful young potato, or a
    not-too-French French bean.
Though the Philistines may jostle, you will rank as an
    apostle in the high æsthetic band,
If you walk down Piccadilly with a poppy or a lily in your
    mediæval hand.

> And every one will say,
> As you walk your flowery way,

"If he's content with a vegetable love which would certainly
    not suit *me*,
Why, what a most particularly pure young man this pure
    young man must be!"

*

THE POLICEMAN'S LOT

When a felon's not engaged in his employment,
    Or maturing his felonious little plans,
His capacity for innocent enjoyment
    Is just as great as any honest man's.
Our feelings we with difficulty smother
    When constabulary duty's to be done:
Ah, take one consideration with another,
    A policeman's lot is not a happy one!

When the enterprising burglar isn't burgling,
    When the cut-throat isn't occupied in crime,
He loves to hear the little brook a-gurgling,
    And listen to the merry village chime.
When the coster's finished jumping on his mother,
    He loves to lie a-basking in the sun:
Ah, take one consideration with another,
    The policeman's lot is not a happy one!

*

THE BRITISH TAR

A British tar is a soaring soul,
    As free as a mountain bird,
His energetic fist should be ready to resist
    A dictatorial word.

His nose should pant and his lip should curl,
His cheeks should flame and his brow should furl,
His bosom should heave and his heart should glow,
And his fist be ever ready for a knock-down blow.

His eyes should flash with an inborn fire,
  His brow with scorn be rung;
He never should bow down to a domineering frown,
  Or the tang of a tyrant tongue.
His foot should stamp and his throat should growl,
His hair should twirl and his face should scowl;
His eyes should flash and his breast protrude,
And this should be his customary attitude!

William Dean Howells

CAPRICE

She hung the cage at the window:
  'If he goes by,' she said,
'He will hear my robin singing,
  And when he lifts his head,
I shall be sitting here to sew,
And he will bow to me, I know.'

The robin sang a love-sweet song,
  The young man raised his head;
The maiden turned away and blushed;
  'I am a fool!' she said,
And went on broidering in silk
A pink-eyed rabbit, white as milk.

The young man loitered slowly
  By the house three times that day;

She took her bird from the window:
  He need not look this way.'
She sat at her piano long,
  And sighed, and played a death-sad song.

But when the day was done, she said,
  'I wish that he would come!
Remember, Mary, if he calls
  Tonight—I'm not at home!'
So when he rang, she went—the elf!—
She went and let him in herself.

Algernon Charles Swinburne

A MATCH

If love were what the rose is,
  And I were like the leaf,
Our lives would grow together
In sad or singing weather,
Blown fields or flowerful closes,
  Green pleasure or gray grief;
If love were what the rose is,
  And I were like the leaf.

If I were what the words are,
  And love were like the tune,
With double sound and single
Delight our lips would mingle,
With kisses glad as birds are
  That get sweet rain at noon;
If I were what the words are,
  And love were like the tune.

If you were life, my darling,
    And I your love were death,
We'd shine and snow together
Ere March made sweet the weather
With daffodil and starling
    And hours of fruitful breath;
If you were life, my darling,
    And I your love were death.

If you were thrall to sorrow,
    And I were page to joy,
We'd play for lives and seasons
With loving looks and treasons
And tears of night and morrow
    And laughs of maid and boy;
If you were thrall to sorrow,
    And I were page to joy.

If you were April's lady
    And I were lord in May,
We'd throw with leaves for hours
And draw for day with flowers,
Till day like night were shady
    And night were bright like day;
If you were April's lady,
    And I were lord in May.

If you were queen of pleasure,
    And I were king of pain,
We'd hunt down love together,
Pluck out his flying-feather,
And teach his feet a measure,
    And find his mouth a rein;
If you were queen of pleasure,
    And I were king of pain.

John Hay

GOOD AND BAD LUCK

Good luck is the gayest of all gay girls,
  Long in one place she will not stay,
Back from your brow she strokes the curls,
  Kisses you quick and flies away.

But Madame Bad Luck soberly comes
  And stays,—no fancy has she for flitting,—
Snatches of true love-songs she hums,
  And sits by your bed, and brings her knitting.
                                    After Heine.

Austin Dobson

TO BRANDER MATTHEWS

[*With a Volume of Verses*]

In vain to-day I scrape and blot:
  The nimble words, the phrases **neat,**
  Decline to mingle or to meet;
My skill is all foregone—forgot.

He will not canter, walk nor trot,
  My Pegasus. I spur, I beat,
              In vain to-day!

And yet 'twere sure the saddest lot
  That I should fail to leave complete
  One poor... the rhyme suggests 'conceit!'
Alas! 'Tis all too clear I'm not
              In *vein* to-day.

ON A FAN THAT BELONGED TO THE MARQUISE DE POMPADOUR

Chicken-skin, delicate, white,
  Painted by Carlo Vanloo,
Loves in a riot of light,
  Roses and vaporous blue;
  Hark to the dainty *frou-frou!*
Picture above, if you can,
  Eyes that could melt as the dew,—
This was the Pompadour's fan!

See how they rise at the sight,
  Thronging the *Œil de Bœuf* through,
Courtiers as butterflies bright,
  Beauties that Fragonard drew,
  Talon-rouge, falbala, queue,
Cardinal, Duke,—to a man,
  Eager to sigh or to sue,—
This was the Pompadour's fan!

Ah, but things more than polite
  Hung on this toy, *voyez-vous!*
Matters of state and of might,
  Things that great ministers do;
  Things that, maybe, overthrew
Those in whose brains they began;
  Here was the sign and the cue,—
This was the Pompadour's fan!

ENVOY

Where are the secrets it knew?
  Weavings of plot and of plan?
  —But where is the Pompadour, too?
This was the Pompadour's *Fan!*

A BALLAD TO QUEEN ELIZABETH
of the Spanish Armada

King Philip had vaunted his claims;
    He had sworn for a year he would sack us;
With an army of heathenish names
    He was coming to fagot and stack us;
    Like the thieves of the sea he would track us,
And shatter our ships on the main;
    But we had bold Neptune to back us,—
And where are the galleons of Spain?

His carackes were christen'd of dames
    To the kirtles whereof he would tack us;
With his saints and his gilded stern-frames,
    He had thought like an egg-shell to crack us:
    Now Howard may get to his Flaccus,
And Drake to his Devon again,
    And Hawkins bowl rubbers to Bacchus,—
For where are the galleons of Spain?

Let his Majesty hang to St. James
    The axe that he whetted to hack us;
He must play at some lustier games
    Or at sea he can hope to out-thwack us;
    To his mines of Peru he would pack us
To tug at his bullet and chain;
    Alas that his Greatness should lack us!—
But where are the galleons of Spain?

Envoy

    GLORIANA!—the Don may attack us
Whenever his stomach he fain;
    He must reach us before he can rack us,...
And where are the galleons of Spain?

DORA *VERSUS* ROSE

'The Case is proceeding.'

From the tragic-est novels at Mudie's—
　　At least, on a practical plan—
To the tales of mere Hodges and Judys,
　　One love is enough for a man.
But no case that I ever yet met is
　　Like mine: I am equally fond
Of Rose, who a charming brunette is,
　　　　　　　And Dora, a blonde.

Each rivals the other in powers—
　　Each waltzes, each warbles, each paints—
Miss Rose, chiefly tumble-down towers;
　　Miss Do., perpendicular saints.
In short, to distinguish is folly;
　　'Twixt the pair I am come to the pass
Of Macheath, between Lucy and Polly,—
　　　　　　　Or Buridan's ass.

If it happens that Rosa I've singled
　　For a soft celebration in rhyme,
Then the ringlets of Dora get mingled
　　Somehow with the tune and the time;
Or I painfully pen me a sonnet
　　To an eyebrow intended to Do.'s,
And behold I am writing upon it
　　　　　　　The legend 'To Rose.'

Or I try to draw Dora (my blotter
　　Is all overscrawled with her head),
If I fancy at last that I've got her,
　　It turns to her rival instead;

Or I find myself placidly adding
  To the rapturous tresses of Rose
Miss Dora's bud-mouth, and her madding,
           Ineffable nose.

Was there ever so sad a dilemma?
  For Rose I would perish (*pro tem.*);
For Dora I'd willingly stem a—
  (Whatever might offer to stem);
But to make the invidious election,—
  To declare that on either one's side
I've a scruple,—a grain, more affection,
         I *cannot* decide.

And, as either so hopelessly nice is,
  My sole and my final resource
Is to wait some indefinite crisis,—
  Some feat of molecular force,
To solve me this riddle conducive
  By no means to peace or repose,
Since the issue can scarce be inclusive
        Of Dora *and* Rose.

(*Afterthought.*)

But, perhaps, if a third (say a Norah),
  Not quite so delightful as Rose,—
Not wholly so charming as Dora,—
  Should appear, is it wrong to suppose,—
As the claims of the others are equal,—
  And flight—in the main—is the best,—
That I might...But no matter,—the sequel
        Is easily guessed.

A KISS

Rose kissed me to-day.
   Will she kiss me to-morrow?
Let it be as it may,
Rose kissed me to-day,
But the pleasure gives way
   To a savour of sorrow;—
Rose kissed me to-day,—
   Will she kiss me to-morrow?

W. N. Ewer

THE CHOSEN PEOPLE

How odd
Of God
To choose
The Jews.

Thomas Hardy

WEATHERS

This is the weather the cuckoo likes,
   And so do I;
When showers betumble the chestnut spikes,
   And nestlings fly:

And the little brown nightingale bills his best,
And they sit outside at "The Travellers' Rest,"
And maids come forth sprig-muslin drest,
And citizens dream of the south and west,
   And so do I.

This is the weather the shepherd shuns,
  And so do I;
When beeches drip in browns and duns,
  And thresh, and ply;
And hill-hid tides throb, throe on throe,
And meadow rivulets overflow,
And drops on gate-bars hang in a row,
And rooks in families homeward go,
  And so do I.

John Addington Symonds

A POEM OF PRIVACY

When a young man, passion-laden,
In a chamber meets a maiden,
  Then felicitous communion,
By love's strain between the twain,
  Grows from forth their union;
For the game, it hath no name,
Of lips, arms, and hidden charms.
            Translated: included in
            Wine, Women and Song

John Payne

A MERRY BALLAD OF VINTNERS

I

By dint of dart, by push of sharpened spear,
  By sweep of scythe or thump of spike-set mace,
By poleaxe, steel-tipped arrow-head or shear
  Of double-handed sword or well-ground ace,
  By dig of dirk or tuck with double face,

Let them be done to death; or let them light
On some ill stead, where brigands lurk by night,
　　That they the hearts from out their breasts may tear,
　　Cut off their heads, then drag them by the hair
And cast them on the dunghill to the swine,
　　That sows and porkers on their flesh may fare,
The vintners that put water in our wine.

II

Let Turkish quarrels run them through the rear
　　And rapiers keen their guts and vitals lace;
Singe their perukes with Greek fire, ay, and sear
　　Their brains with levins; string them brace by brace
　　Up to the gibbet; or for greater grace,
Let gout and dropsy slay the knaves outright:
Or else let drive into each felon wight
　　Irons red-heated in the furnace-flare:
　　Let half a score of hangmen flay them bare;
And on the morrow, seethed in oil or brine,
　　Let four great horses rend them then and there,
The vintners that put water in our wine.

III

Let some great gunshot blow their heads off sheer;
　　Let thunders catch them in the market-place;
Let rend their limbs and cast them far and near,
　　For dogs to batten on their bodies base;
　　Or let the lightning-stroke their sight efface.
Frost, hail and snow let still upon them bite;
Strip off their clothes and leave them naked quite,
　　For rain to drench them in the open air;
　　Lard them with knives and poniards and then bear

Their carrion forth and soak it in the Rhine;
  Break all their bones with mauls and do not spare
The vintners that put water in our wine.

ENVOI

Prince, may God curse their vitals! is my prayer;
  And may they burst with venom all, in fine,
These traitorous thieves, accursèd and unfair,
  The vintners that put water in our wine.

*Translated from the French of
François Villon*

Barry Pain

MARTIN LUTHER AT POTSDAM

What lightning shall light it? What thunder shall tell it?
  In the height of the height, in the depth of the deep?
Shall the sea-storm declare it, or paint it, or smell it?
  Shall the price of a slave be its treasure to keep?
When the night has grown near with the gems on her
    bosom,
  When the white of mine eyes is the whiteness of snow,
When the cabman—in liquor—drives a blue roan, a kicker,
  Into the land of the dear long ago.

Ah!—Ah, again!—You will come to me, fall on me—
  You are *so* heavy, and I am *so* flat.
And I? I shall not be at home when you call on me,
  But stray down the wind like a gentleman's hat:
I shall list to the stars when the music is purple,
  Be drawn through a pipe, and exhaled into rings;
Turn to sparks, and then straightway get stuck in the gate-
    way
  That stands between speech and unspeakable things.

As I mentioned before, by what light is it lighted?
　　Oh! Is it fourpence, or piebald, or gray?
Is it a mayor that a mother has knighted,
　　Or is it a horse of the sun and the day?
Is it a pony? If so, who will change it?
　　O golfer, be quiet, and mark where it scuds,
And think of its paces—of owners and races—
　　Relinquish the links for the study of studs.

Not understood? Take me hence! Take me yonder!
　　Take me away to the land of my rest—
There where the Ganges and other gees wander,
　　And uncles and antelopes act for the best,
And all things are mixed and run into each other
　　In a violet twilight of virtues and sins,
With the church-spires below you and no one to show you
　　Where the curate leaves off and the pew-rent begins!

In the black night through the rank grass the snakes peer—
　　The cobs and the cobras are partial to grass—
And a boy wanders out with a knowledge of Shakespeare
　　That's not often found in a boy of his class,
And a girl wanders out without any knowledge,
　　And a bird wanders out, and a cow wanders out,
Likewise one wether, and they wander together—
　　There's a good deal of wandering lying about.

But it's all for the best; I've been told by my friends, Sir,
　　That in verses I'd written the meaning was slight;
I've tried with no meaning—to make 'em amends, Sir—
　　And find that this kind's still more easy to write.
The title has nothing to do with the verses,
　　But think of the millions—the laborers who
In busy employment find deepest enjoyment,
　　And yet, like my title, have nothing to do!

Anonymous

A CENTIPEDE WAS HAPPY QUITE

A centipede was happy quite,
    Until a frog in fun
Said, "Pray, which leg comes after which?"
This raised her mind to such a pitch,
She lay distracted in the ditch
    Considering how to run.

Walter Learned

AN EXPLANATION

Her lips were so near
    That what—else could I do?
You'll be angry, I fear,
But her lips were so near—
Well, I can't make it clear,
    Or explain it to you,
But—her lips were so near
    That—what else could I do?

William Ernest Henley

BALLADE OF DEAD ACTORS

To E. J. H.

Where are the passions they essayed,
And where the tears they made to flow?
Where the wild humours they portrayed
For laughing worlds to see and know?
Othello's wrath and Juliet's woe?
Sir Peter's whims and Timon's gall?

And Millamant and Romeo?
Into the night go one and all.

Where are the braveries, fresh or frayed?
The plumes, the armours—friend and foe?
The cloth of gold, the rare brocade,
The mantles glittering to and fro?
The pomp, the pride, the royal show?
The cries of war and festival?
The youth, the grace, the charm, the glow?
Into the night go one and all.

The curtain falls, the play is played:
The Beggar packs beside the Beau;
The Monarch troops, and troops the Maid;
The Thunder huddles with the Snow.
Where are the revellers high and low?
The clashing swords? The lover's call?
The dancers gleaming row on row?
Into the night go one and all.

ENVOY

Prince, in one common overthrow
The Hero tumbles with the Thrall:
As dust that drives, as straws that blow,
Into the night go one and all.

Dean Henry Aldrich

WHY I DRINK

If on my theme I rightly think,
There are five reasons why I drink,—
Good wine, a friend, because I'm dry,
Or lest I should be by and by,
Or any other reason why.

Ben King

THE PESSIMIST

Nothing to do but work,
  Nothing to eat but food,
Nothing to wear but clothes
  To keep one from going nude.

Nothing to breathe but air,
  Quick as a flash 't is gone;
Nowhere to fall but off,
  Nowhere to stand but on.

Nothing to comb but hair,
  Nowhere to sleep but in bed,
Nothing to weep but tears,
  Nothing to bury but dead.

Nothing to sing but songs,
  Ah, well, alas! alack!
Nowhere to go but out,
  Nowhere to come but back.

Nothing to see but sights,
  Nothing to quench but thirst,
Nothing to have but what we've got;
  Thus thro' life we are cursed.

Nothing to strike but a gait;
  Everything moves that goes.
Nothing at all but common sense
  Can ever withstand these woes.

Eugene Field

HORACE I, 11

Seek not, Lucome, to know how long you're going to live
    yet—
What boons the gods will yet withhold, or what they're
    going to give yet;
For Jupiter will have his way, despite how much we worry—
Some will hang on for many a day and some die in a
    hurry,
The wisest thing for you to do is to embark this diem
Upon a merry escapade with some such bard as I am;
And while we sport, I'll reel you off such odes as shall
    surprise ye—
To-morrow, when the headache comes—well, then I'll
    satirize ye!

Henry Cuyler Bunner

BEHOLD THE DEEDS!

(Being the plaint of Adolphe Culpepper Ferguson, Salesman of Fancy Notions, held in durance of his Landlady for a "failure to connect" on a Saturday night.)

I would that all men my case would know,
    How grievously I suffer for no sin:
I, Adolphe Culpepper Ferguson, for lo!
    I of my landlady am lockèd in
For being short on this sad Saturday,
Nor having shekels of silver wherewith to pay:

She turned and is departed with my key;
Wherefore, not even as other boarders free,
   I sing (as prisoners to their dungeon-stones
When for ten days they expiate a spree):
     Behold the deeds that are done of Mrs. Jones!

One night and one day have I wept my woe;
   Nor wot I, when the morrow doth begin
If I shall have to write to Briggs & Co.,
   To pray them to advance the requisite tin
For ransom of their salesman, that he may
Go forth as other boarders go alway—
As those I hear now flocking from their tea,
Led by the daughter of my landlady
   Piano-ward. This day, for all my moans,
Dry-bread and water have been servèd me.
     Behold the deeds that are done of Mrs. Jones!

Miss Amabel Jones is musical, and so
   The heart of the young he-boarder doth win,
Playing "The Maiden's Prayer" *adagio*—
   That fetcheth him, as fetcheth the "bunko skin"
The innocent rustic. For my part, I pray
That Badarjewska maid may wait for aye
Ere sits she with a lover, as did we
Once sit together, Amabel! Can it be
   That all that arduous wooing not atones
For Saturday's shortness of trade dollars three?
     Behold the deeds that are done of Mrs. Jones!

Yea! She forgets that arm that was wont to go
   Around her waist. She wears a buckle whose pin
Galleth the crook of her young man's elbow.
   I forget not, for I that youth have been!

Smith was aforetime the Lothario gay.
Yet once, I mind me, Smith was forced to stay
Close in his room. Not calm as I was he;
But his noise brought no pleasurance, verily.
  Small ease he got of playing on the bones
Or hammering on the stove-pipe, that I see.
  Behold the deeds that are done of Mrs. Jones!

Thou, for whose fear the figurative crow
  I eat, accursed be thou and all thy kind!
Thee I will show up—yea, up I will show
  Thy too-thick buckwheats and thy tea too thin.
Ay! here I dare thee, ready for the fray:
Thou dost *not* "keep a first-class house," I say!
It does not with the advertisements agree.
Thou lodgest a Briton with a puggaree,
  And thou hast harbored Jacobses and Cohns,
Also a Mulligan. Thus denounce I thee!
  Behold the deeds that are done of Mrs. Jones!

ENVOY

Boarders! the worst I have not told to ye:
She hath stolen my trousers, that I may not flee
  Privily by the window. Hence these groans.
There is no fleeing in a *robe de nuit*.
  Behold the deeds that are done of Mrs. Jones!

*

SHAKE, MULLEARY AND GO-ETHE

I

I have a bookcase, which is what
Many much better men have not.
There are no books inside, for books,
I am afraid, might spoil its looks.

But I've three busts, all second-hand,
Upon the top. You understand
I could not put them underneath—
Shake, Mulleary and Go-ethe.

II

Shake was a dramatist of note;
He lived by writing things to quote.
He long ago put on his shroud;
Some of his works are rather loud.
His bald-spot's dusty, I suppose.
I know there's dust upon his nose.
I'll have to give each nose a sheath—
Shake, Mulleary and Go-ethe.

III

Mulleary's line was quite the same;
He has more hair, but far less fame.
I would not from that fame retrench—
But he is foreign, being French.
Yet high his haughty head he heaves,
The only one done up in leaves,
They're rather limited on wreath—
Shake, Mulleary and Go-ethe.

IV

Go-ethe wrote in the German tongue:
He must have learned it very young.
His nose is quite a butt for scoff,
Although an inch of it is off.
He did quite nicely for the Dutch;
But here he doesn't count for much.
They sit there, on their chests, as bland
Shake, Mulleary and Go-ethe.

v

They all are off their native heath—
As if they were not second-hand.
I do not know of what they think,
Nor why they never frown or wink.
But why from smiling they refrain
I think I clearly can explain:
They none of them could show much teeth—
Shake, Mulleary and Go-ethe.

Colonel D. Streamer
(R. H. Russell)

TENDER-HEARTEDNESS

Little Willie, in the best of sashes,
Fell in the fire and was burned to ashes.
By and by the room grew chilly,
But no one liked to poke up Willie.

*

AUNT ELIZA

In the drinking-well
    (Which the plumber built her)
Aunt Eliza fell,—
    We must buy a filter.

Anonymous

GREAT FLEAS

Great fleas have little fleas upon their back to bite 'em,
And little fleas have lesser fleas, and so *ad infinitum*.
The great fleas themselves in turn have greater fleas to go on,
While these again have greater still, and greater still, and so
    on.

Edward Sanford Martin

INFIRM

'I will not go,' he said, 'for well
I know her eyes' insidious spell,
And how unspeakably he feels
Who takes no pleasure in his meals.
I know a one-idea'd man
Should undergo the social ban,
And if she once my purpose melts
I know I'll think of nothing else.

'I care not though her teeth are pearls—
The town is full of nicer girls!
I care not though her lips are red—
It does not do to lose one's head!
I'll give her leisure to discover,
For once, how little I think of her;
And then, how will she feel?' cried he—
And took his hat and went to see.

Bliss Carman

IN PHILISTIA

Of all the places on the map,
Some queer and others queerer,
Arcadia is dear to me,
Philistia is dearer.

There dwell the few who never knew
The pangs of heavenly hunger,
As fresh and fair and fond and frail
As when the world was younger.

If there is any sweeter sound
Than bobolinks or thrushes,
It is the frou-frou of their silks—
The roll of their barouches.

I love them even when they're good,
As well as when they're sinners—
When they are sad and worldly wise
And when they are beginners.

(I say I do; of course the fact,
For better or for worse, is,
My unerratic life denies
My too erotic verses.)

I dote upon their waywardness,
Their foibles and their follies.
If there's a madder pate than Di's,
Perhaps it may be Dolly's.

They have no "problems" to discuss,
No "theories" to discover;
They are not "new;" and I—I am
Their very grateful lover.

I care not if their minds confuse
Alastor with Aladdin;
And Cimabue is far less
To them than Chimmie Fadden.

They never heard of William Blake,
Nor saw a Botticelli;
Yet one is, "Yours till death, Louise,"
And one, "Your loving Nelly."

They never tease me for my views,
Nor tax me with my grammar;
Nor test me on the latest news,
Until I have to stammer.

They never talk about their "moods,"
They never know they have them;
The world is good enough for them,
And that is why I love them.

They never puzzle me with Greek,
Nor drive me mad with Ibsen;
Yet over forms as fair as Eve's
They wear the gowns of Gibson.

Sir Owen Seaman

THE USES OF OCEAN

[Lines written in an irresponsible holiday mood.]

To people who allege that we
Incline to overrate the Sea
I answer, "We do not;
Apart from being coloured blue,

It has its uses not a few;
I cannot think what we should do
   If ever 'the deep did rot.' "

Take ships, for instance. You will note
That, lacking stuff on which to float,
   They could not get about;
Dreadnought and liner, smack and yawl,
And other types that you'll recall—
They simply could not sail at all
   If Ocean once gave out.

And see the trouble which it saves
To islands; but for all those waves
   That made us what we are—
But for their help so kindly lent,
Europe could march right through to Kent
And never need to circumvent
   A single British tar.

Take fish, again. I have in mind
No better field that they could find
   For exercise and sport;
How would the whale, I want to know,
The blubbery whale contrive to blow?
Where would your playful kipper go
   If the supply ran short?

And hence we rank the Ocean high;
But there are privy reasons why
   Its praise is on my lip:
I deem it, when my heart is set
On walking into something wet,
The nicest medium I have met
   In which to take a dip.

Rudyard Kipling

THE LADIES

I've taken my fun where I've found it;
  I've rogued an' I've ranged in my time;
I've 'ad my pickin' o' sweethearts,
  An' four o' the lot was prime.
One was an 'arf-caste widow,
  One was a woman at Prome,
One was the wife of a jemadar-sais,
  An' one is a girl at 'ome.

Now I aren't no 'and with the ladies,
  For, takin' 'em all along,
You never can say till you've tried 'em
  An' then you are like to be wrong.
There's times when you'll think that you mightn't,
  There's times when you'll know that you might;
But the things you will learn from the Yellow and Brown,
  They'll 'elp you a lot with the White!

I was a young un at 'Oogli,
  Shy as a girl to begin;
Aggie de Castrer she made me,
  An' Aggie was clever as sin;
Older than me, but my first un—
  More like a mother she were—
Showed me the way to promotion an' pay,
  An' I learned about women from 'er!

Then I was ordered to Burma,
  Actin' in charge o' Bazar,
An' I got me a tiddy live 'eathen
  Through buyin' supplies off 'er pa.

Funny an' yellow an' faithful—
   Doll in a teacup she were,
But we lived on the square, like a true-married pair,
   An' I learned about women from 'er!

Then we was shifted to Neemuch
   (Or I might ha' been keepin' 'er now),
An' I took with a shiny she-devil,
   The wife of a nigger at Mhow;
'Taught me the gipsy-folks bolee;
   Kind o' volcano she were,
For she knifed me one night 'cause I wished she was white,
   And learned about women from 'er!

Then I come 'ome in a trooper,
   'Long of a kid o' sixteen—
'Girl from a convent at Meerut,
   The straightest I ever 'ave seen.
Love at first sight was 'er trouble,
   She didn't know what it were;
An' I wouldn't do such, 'cause I liked 'er too much,
   But—I learned about women from 'er!

I've taken my fun where I've found it,
   An' now I must pay for my fun,
For the more you 'ave known o' the others
   The less will you settle to one;
An' the end of it's sittin' and thinkin',
   An' dreamin' Hell-fires to see;
So be warned by my lot (which I know you will not),
An' learn about women from me!

What did the Colonel's Lady think?
   Nobody ever knew.

Somebody asked the Sergeant's Wife,
  An' she told 'em true!
When you get to a man in the case,
  They're like as a row of pins—
For the Colonel's Lady an' Judy O'Grady
  Are sisters under their skins!

Gelett Burgess

I WISH THAT MY ROOM HAD A FLOOR

I wish that my room had a floor;
I don't so much care for a door,
    But this walking around
    Without touching the ground
Is getting to be such a bore.

George Ade

R-E-M-O-R-S-E

The cocktail is a pleasant drink,
It's mild and harmless, I don't think.
When you've had one, you call for two,
And then you don't care what you do.
Last night I hoisted twenty-three
Of these arrangements into me;
My wealth increased, I swelled with pride;
I was pickled, primed and ossified.
    R-E-M-O-R-S-E!
Those dry martinis did the work for me;
Last night at twelve I felt immense;
To-day I feel like thirty cents.

At four I sought my whirling bed,
At eight I woke with such a head!
It is no time for mirth or laughter—
The cold, grey dawn of the morning after.

If ever I want to sign the pledge,
It's the morning after I've had an edge;
When I've been full of the oil of joy
And fancied I was a sporty boy.
This world was one kaleidoscope
Of purple bliss, transcended hope.
But now I'm feeling mighty blue—
Three cheers for the W. C. T. U.!
    R-E-M-O-R-S-E!
The water wagon is the place for me;
I think that somewhere in the game,
I wept and told my maiden name.

My eyes are bleared, my coppers hot;
I try to eat, but I can not;
It is no time for mirth or laughter—
The cold, grey dawn of the morning after.

Bert Leston Taylor

CANOPUS

When quacks with pills political would dope us,
    When politics absorbs the livelong day,
I like to think about that star Canopus,
    So far, so far away.

Greatest of visioned suns, they say who list 'em;
    To weigh its science almost must despair.
Its shell would hold our whole dinged solar system,
    Nor even know 'twas there.

When temporary chairmen utter speeches,
  And frenzied henchmen howl their battle hymns,
My thoughts float out across the cosmic reaches
  To where Canopus swims.

When men are calling names and making faces,
  And all the world's ajangle and ajar,
I meditate on interstellar spaces
  And smoke a mild seegar.

For after one has had about a week of
  The argument of friends as well as foes,
A star that has no parallax to speak of
  Conduces to repose.

*

THE LAZY WRITER

  In summer I'm disposed to shirk,
  As summer is no time to work.

  In winter inspiration dies
  For lack of out-door exercise.

  In spring I'm seldom in the mood,
  Because of vernal lassitude.

  The fall remains. But such a fall!
  We've really had no fall at all.

H. H. Bashford

WHERE DO THE GIPSIES COME FROM?

  Where do the gipsies come from?
  The gipsies come from Egypt.
  The fiery sun begot them,
    Their dam was the desert dry.

She lay there stripped and basking,
And gave them suck for the asking,
And an Emperor's bone to play with,
  Whenever she heard them cry.

What did the gipsies do there?
They built a tomb for Pharaoh,
They built a tomb for Pharaoh,
  So tall it touched the sky.
They buried him deep inside it,
Then let what would betide it,
They saddled their lean-ribbed ponies
  And left him there to die.

What do the gipsies do now?
They follow the Sun, their father,
They follow the Sun, their father,
  They know not whither nor why.
Whatever they find they take it,
And if it's the law they break it.
So never you talk to a gipsy,
  Or look in a gipsy's eye.

Carolyn Wells

A POSSIBILITY

I only kissed her hand;
  Is that why Lisette dislikes me?
I cannot understand—
I only kissed her hand,
I deserved a reprimand;—
  But another notion strikes me:
I only kissed her *hand;*
  Is that why Lisette dislikes me?

Anthony C. Deane

THE BALLAD OF THE *BILLYCOCK*

It was the good ship *Billycock,* with thirteen men aboard,
  Athirst to grapple with their country's foes,—
A crew, 'twill be admitted, not numerically fitted
  To navigate a battleship in prose.

It was the good ship *Billycock* put out from Plymouth Sound,
  While lustily the gallant heroes cheered,
And all the air was ringing with the merry bo'sun's singing,
  Till in the gloom of night she disappeared.

But when the morning broke on her, behold, a dozen ships,
  A dozen ships of France around her lay,
(Or, if that isn't plenty, I will gladly make it twenty),
  And hemmed her close in Salamander Bay.

Then to the Lord High Admiral there spake a cabin-boy:
  "Methinks," he said, "the odds are somewhat great,
And, in the present crisis, a cabin-boy's advice is
  That you and France had better arbitrate!"

"Pooh!" said the Lord High Admiral, and slapped his manly
      chest,
  "Pooh! That would be both cowardly and wrong;
Shall I, a gallant fighter, give the needy ballad-writer
  No suitable material for song?"

"Nay—is the shorthand-writer here?—I tell you, one and all,
  I mean to do my duty, as I ought;
With eager satisfaction let us clear the decks for action
  And fight the craven Frenchmen!" So they fought.

And (after several stanzas which as yet are incomplete,
    Describing all the fight in epic style)
When the *Billycock* was going, she'd a dozen prizes towing
    (Or twenty, as above) in single file!

Ah, long in glowing English hearts the story will remain,
    The memory of that historic day,
And, while we rule the ocean, we will picture with emotion
    The *Billycock* in Salamander Bay!

P.S.—I've lately noticed that the critics—who, I think,
    In praising *my* productions are remiss—
Quite easily are captured, and profess themselves enraptured,
    By patriotic ditties such as this,

For making which you merely take the same dauntless Eng-
    lishmen,
    Guns, heroism, slaughter and a fleet—
Ingredients you mingle in a metre with a jingle,
    And there you have your masterpiece complete!

Why, then, with labour infinite, produce a book of verse
    To languish on the "All for Twopence" shelf?
The ballad bold and breezy comes particularly easy—
    I mean to take to writing it myself!

Hilaire Belloc

THE YAK

As a friend to the children commend me the yak,
    You will find it exactly the thing:
It will carry and fetch, you can ride on its back,
    Or lead it about with a string.

A Tartar who dwells on the plains of Thibet
    (A desolate region of snow)
Has for centuries made it a nursery pet,
    And surely the Tartar should know!

Then tell your papa where the Yak can be got,
    And if he is awfully rich,
He will buy you the creature—or else he will not,
    (I cannot be positive which).

*

THEY SAY, AND I AM GLAD THEY SAY

They say, and I am glad they say,
    It is so; and it may be so,
It may be just the other way,
    I cannot tell, but this I know—
From quiet homes and first beginnings
    Out to the undiscovered ends
There's nothing worth the wear of winning
    Save laughter and the love of friends.

Arthur Guiterman

THE LEGEND OF THE FIRST CAM-U-EL

An Arabian Apologue

Across the sands of Syria,
    Or, possibly, Algeria,
Or some benighted neighborhood of barrenness and drouth,
    There came the Prophet Sam-u-el
    Upon the Only Cam-u-el—
A bumpy, grumpy Quadruped of discontented mouth.

The atmosphere was glutinous;
    The Cam-u-el was mutinous;
He dumped the pack from off his back; with horrid grunts
        and squeals
    He made the desert hideous;
    With strategy perfidious
He tied his neck in curlicues, he kicked his paddy heels.

    Then quoth the gentle Sam-u-el,
    "You rogue, I ought to lam you well!
Though zealously I've shielded you from every grief and
        woe,
    It seems, to voice a platitude,
    You haven't any gratitude.
I'd like to hear what cause you have for doing thus and so!"

    To him replied the Cam-u-el,
    "I beg your pardon, Sam-u-el.
I know that I'm a Reprobate. I know that I'm a Freak;
    But, oh! this utter loneliness!
    My too-distinguished Onliness!
Were there but other Cam-u-els I wouldn't be Unique."

    The Prophet beamed beguilingly.
    "Aha," he answered, smilingly,
"You feel the need of company? I clearly understand.
    We'll speedily create for you
    The corresponding mate for you—
Ho! presto, change-o, dinglebat!"—he waved a potent hand,

    And, lo! from out Vacuity
    A second Incongruity,
To wit, a Lady Cam-u-el was born through magic art.

Her structure anatomical,
　Her form and face were comical;
She was, in short, a Cam-u-el, the other's counterpart.

　　As Spaniards gaze on Aragon,
　　Upon that Female Paragon
So gazed the Prophet's Cam-u-el, that primal Desert Ship.
　　A connoisseur meticulous,
　　He found her that ridiculous
He grinned from ear to auricle *until he split his lip!*

　　Because of his temerity
　　That Cam-u-el's posterity
Must wear divided upper lips through all their solemn lives!
　　A prodigy astonishing
　　Reproachfully admonishing
Those wicked, heartless married men who ridicule their
　　　　wives.

Anonymous

CONVERSATIONAL

"How's your father?" came the whisper,
　Bashful Ned the silence breaking;
"Oh, he's nicely," Annie murmured,
　Smilingly the question taking.

Conversation flagged a moment,
　Hopeless Ned essayed another:
"Annie, I—I," then a coughing,
　And the question, "How's your mother?"

"Mother? Oh, she's doing finely!"
  Fleeting fast was all forbearance,
When in low, despairing accents,
  Came the climax, "How's your parents?"

Walter de la Mare

TIRED TIM

Poor tired Tim! It's sad for him.
He lags the long bright morning through,
Ever so tired of nothing to do;
He moons and mopes the livelong day,
Nothing to think about, nothing to say;
Up to bed with his candle to creep,
Too tired to yawn; too tired to sleep:
Poor tired Tim! It's sad for him.

Keith Preston

AN ORIGINAL CUSS

A real original, I think,
  My friend Bill can be termed;
A smoker, not inveterate,
  A drinker, not confirmed,

A hail fellow, but not well met,
  A realtor, but no Babbitt;
I never knew a cuss like Bill
  For cutting loose from habit.

Guy Wetmore Carryl

THE INHUMAN WOLF
and
THE LAMB SANS GENE

A gaunt and relentless wolf, possessed
  Of a quite insatiable thirst,
Once paused at a stream to drink and rest,
And found that, bound on a similar quest,
  A lamb had arrived there first.

The lamb was a lamb of a garrulous mind
  And frivolity most extreme:
In the fashion common to all his kind,
He cantered in front and galloped behind,
  And troubled the limpid stream.

"My friend," said the wolf, with a winsome air,
  "Your capers I can't admire."
"Go to!" quoth the lamb. (Though he said not where,
He showed what he meant by his brazen stare
And the way that he gambolled higher.)

"My capers," he cried, "are the kind that are
  Invariably served with lamb.
Remember, this is a public bar,
And I'll do as I please. If your drink I mar,
  I don't give a tinker's ——."

He paused and glanced at the rivulet,
  And that pause than speech was worse,
For his roving eye a saw-mill met,
And, near it, the word which should be set
  At the end of the previous verse.

Said the wolf: "You are tough and may bring remorse,
  But of such is the world well rid.
I've swallowed your capers, I've swallowed your sauçe,
And it's plain to be seen that my only course
  Is swallowing you." He did.

THE MORAL: The wisest lambs they are
  Who, when they're assailed by thirst,
Keep well away from a public bar;
For of all black sheep, or near, or far,
  The public bar-lamb's worst!

*

LITTLE BOY BLUE

Composing scales beside the rails
  That flanked a field of corn,
A farmer's boy with vicious joy
  Performed upon a horn:
The vagrant airs, the fragrant airs
  Around that field that strayed,
Took flight before the flagrant airs
  That noisome urchin played.

He played with care "The Maiden's Prayer";
  He played "God Save the Queen,"
"Die Wacht am Rhein," and "Auld Lang Syne,"
  And "Wearing of the Green":
With futile toots, and brutal toots,
  And shrill chromatic scales,
And utterly inutile toots,
  And agonizing wails.

The while he played, around him strayed,
  And calmly chewed the cud,
Some thirty-nine assorted kine,
  All ankle-deep in mud:
They stamped about and tramped about
  That mud, till all the troupe
Made noises, as they ramped about,
  Like school-boys eating soup.

Till, growing bored, with one accord
  They broke the fence forlorn:
The field was doomed. The cows consumed
  Two-thirds of all the corn,
And viciously, maliciously,
  Went prancing o'er the loam.
That landscape expeditiously
  Resembled harvest-home.

"Most idle ass of all your class,"
  The farmer said with scorn:
"Just see, my son, what you have done!
  The cows are in the corn!"
"Oh drat," he said, "the brat!" he said.
  The cowherd seemed to rouse.
"My friend, it's worse than that," he said.
  "The corn is in the cows."

The MORAL lies before our eyes.
  When tending kine and corn,
Don't spend your noons in tooting tunes
  Upon a blatant horn:
Or scaling, and assailing, and
  With energy immense,
Your cows will take a railing, and
  The farmer take offense.

HOW JACK FOUND THAT BEANS MAY GO
BACK ON A CHAP

Without the slightest basis
For hypochondriasis
  A widow had forebodings
            which a cloud around her flung,
And with expression cynical
For half the day a clinical
  Thermometer she held
            beneath her tongue.

When'er she read the papers
She suffered from the vapors,
  At every tale of malady
            or accident she'd groan;
In every new and smart disease,
From housemaid's knee to heart disease,
  She recognized the symptoms
            as her own!

She had a yearning chronic
To try each novel tonic,
  Elixir, panacea, lotion,
            opiate, and balm;
And from a homeopathist
Would change to an hydropathist,
  And back again,
            with stupefying calm!

She was nervous, cataleptic,
And anemic, and dyspeptic:
  Though not convinced of apoplexy,
            yet she had her fears.

She dwelt with force fanatical
Upon a twinge rheumatical,
  And said she had a
               buzzing in her ears!

Now all of this bemoaning
And this grumbling and this groaning
  The mind of Jack, her son and heir,
               unconscionably bored.
His heart completely hardening,
He gave his time to gardening,
  For raising beans was
               something he adored.

Each hour in accents morbid
This limp maternal bore bid
  Her callous son affectionate
             and lachrymose good-bys.
She never granted Jack a day
Without some long "Alackaday!"
  Accompanied by
               rolling of the eyes.

But Jack, no panic showing,
Just watched his beanstalk growing,
  And twined with tender fingers
             the tendrils up the pole.
At all her words funereal
He smiled a smile ethereal,
  Or sighed an absent-minded
             "Bless my soul!"

That hollow-hearted creature
Would never change a feature:
  No tear bedimmed his eye, however
             touching was her talk.

She never fussed or flurried him,
The only thing that worried him
   Was when no bean-pods
                grew upon the stalk\)

But then he wabbled loosely
His head, and wept profusely,
   And, taking out his handkerchief
              to mop away his tears,
Exclaimed: "It hasn't got any!"
He found this blow to botany
   Was sadder than were all
              his mother's fears.

The Moral is that gardeners pine
Whene'er no pods adorn the vine.
Of all sad words experience gleans
The saddest are: "It *might* have beans."
   (I did not make this up myself:
   'Twas in a book upon my shelf.
   It's witty, but I don't deny
   It's rather Whittier than I!)

G. K. Chesterton

FEAST ON WINE OR FAST ON WATER

Feast on wine or fast on water,
   And your honor shall stand sure;
God Almighty's son and daughter,
   He the valiant, she the pure.
If an angel out of heaven
   Brings you other things to drink,
Thank him for his kind intentions,
   Go and pour them down the sink.

Tea is like the East he grows in,
  A great yellow Mandarin,
With urbanity of manner,
  And unconsciousness of sin;
All the women, like a harem,
  At his pig-tail troop along,
And, like all the East he grows in,
  He is Poison when he's strong.

Tea, although an Oriental,
  Is a gentleman at least;
Cocoa is a cad and coward,
  Cocoa is a vulgar beast;
Cocoa is a dull, disloyal,
  Lying, crawling cad and clown,
And may very well be grateful
  To the fool that takes him down.

As for all the windy waters,
  They were rained like trumpets down,
When good drink had been dishonoured
  By the tipplers of the town.
When red wine had brought red ruin,
  And the death-dance of our times,
Heaven sent us Soda Water
  As a torment for our crimes.

*

COMMERCIAL CANDOUR

(On the outside of a sensational novel is printed the statement: "The back of the cover will tell you the plot.")

Our fathers to creed and tradition were tied,
They opened a book to see what was inside,

And of various methods they deemed not the worst
Was to find the first chapter and look at it first.
And so from the first to the second they passed,
Till in servile routine they arrived at the last.
But a literate age, unbenighted by creed,
Can find on two boards all it wishes to read;
For the front of the cover shows somebody shot
And the back of the cover will tell you the plot.

Between, that the book may be handily padded,
Some pages of mere printed matter are added,
Expanding the theme, which in case of great need
The curious reader might very well read
With the zest that is lent to a game worth the winning,
By knowing the end when you start the beginning;
While our barbarous sires, who would read every word
With a morbid desire to find out what occurred
Went drearily drudging through Dickens and Scott.
But the back of the cover will tell you the plot.

The wild village folk in earth's earliest prime
Could often sit still for an hour at a time
And hear a blind beggar, nor did the tale pall
Because Hector must fight before Hector could fall:
Nor was Scheherazade required, at the worst,
To tell her tales backwards and finish them first;
And the minstrels who sang about battle and banners
Found the rude camp-fire crowd had some notion of
    manners.
Till Forster (who pelted the people like crooks,
The Irish with buckshot, the English with books),
Established the great educational scheme
Of compulsory schooling, that glorious theme.

Some learnt how to read, and the others forgot,
And the back of the cover will tell you the plot.

O Genius of Business! O marvellous brain,
Come in place of the priests and the warriors to reign!
O Will to Get On that makes everything go—
O Hustle! O Pep! O Publicity! O!
Shall I spend three-and-sixpence to purchase the book,
Which we all can pick up on the bookstall and look?
Well, it may appear strange, but I think I shall not,
For the back of the cover will tell you the plot.

*

A BALLADE OF SUICIDE

The gallows in my garden, people say,
Is new and neat and adequately tall.
I tie the noose on in a knowing way
As one that knots his necktie for a ball;
But just as all the neighbours—on the wall—
Are drawing a long breath to shout "Hurray!"
The strangest whim has seized me. ... After all
I think I will not hang myself to-day.

To-morrow is the time I get my pay—
My uncle's sword is hanging in the hall—
I see a little cloud all pink and grey—
Perhaps the Rector's mother will *not* call—
I fancy that I heard from Mr. Gall
That mushrooms could be cooked another way—
I never read the works of Juvenal—
I think I will not hang myself to-day.

The world will have another washing day;
The decadents decay; the pedants pall;
And H. G. Wells has found that children play,
And Bernard Shaw discovered that they squall;
Rationalists are growing rational—
And through thick woods one finds a stream astray,
So secret that the very sky seems small—
I think I will not hang myself to-day.

ENVOI

Prince, I can hear the trumpet of Germinal,
The tumbrils toiling up the terrible way;
Even to-day your royal head may fall—
I think I will not hang myself to-day.

*

THE SONG AGAINST SONGS

The song of the sorrow of Melisande is a weary song and a
    dreary song,
The glory of Mariana's grange had got into great decay,
The song of the Raven Never More has never been called a
    cheery song,
And the brightest things in Baudelaire are anything else but
    gay.

But who will write us a riding song
Or a hunting song or a drinking song,
Fit for them that arose and rode
When day and the wine were red?
But bring me a quart of claret out,
And I will write you a clinking song,
A song of war and a song of wine
And a song to wake the dead.

The song of the fury of Fragolette is a florid song and a
    torrid song,
The song of the sorrow of Tara is sung to a harp unstrung,
The song of the cheerful Shropshire Lad I consider a per-
    fectly horrid song,
And the song of the happy Futurist is a song that can't be
    sung.

But who will write us a riding song
Or a fighting song or a drinking song,
Fit for the fathers of you and me,
That know how to think and thrive?
But the song of Beauty and Art and Love
Is simply an utterly stinking song,
To double you up and drag you down
And damn your soul alive.

E. G. V. Knox

TO THE GOD OF LOVE

Come to me, Eros, if you needs must come
    This year, with milder twinges;
Aim not your arrow at the bull's-eye plumb,
But let the outer pericardium
    Be where the point impinges.

Garishly beautiful I watch them wane
    Like sunsets in a pink west,
The passions of the past; but O their pain!
You recollect that nice affair with Jane?
    We nearly had an inquest.

I want some mellower romance than these,
    Something that shall not waken

The bosom of the bard from midnight ease,
Nor spoil his appetite for breakfast, please
   (Porridge and eggs and bacon.)

Something that shall not steep the soul in gall,
   Nor plant it *in excelsis,*
Nor quite prevent the bondman in its thrall
From biffing off the tee as good a ball
   As anybody else's;

But rather, when the world is dull and gray
   And everything seems horrid,
And books are impotent to charm away
The leaden-footed hours, shall make me say,
   "My hat!" (and strike my forehead)

"I am in love, O circumstance how sweet!
   O ne'er to be forgot knot!"
And praise the damsel's eyebrows, and repeat
Her name out loud, until it's time to eat,
   Or go to bed, or what not.

This is the kind of desultory bolt,
   Eros, I bid you shoot me;
One with no barb to agitate and jolt,
One where the feathers have begun to moult—
   Any old sort will suit me.

Don Marquis

THE JOKESMITH'S VACATION

What did I do on my blooming vacation?
   I solemnly ate, and I frequently slept;
But I chiefly live over in fond contemplation
   The days that I wept. For I wept and I wept.

One making his living by humorous sallies
  Finds the right to be mournful a blessed relief—
And hour after hour in the byways and alleys
  I sobbed out my soul in a passion of grief.

I'm really not humorous. (Cue to be scornful,
  Dear reader, and murmur, "We know that you ain't!")
And gee! what a treat to be human and mournful,
  As glum as a gumboil, as sad as a saint!

Any one can weep tears when he suffers abrasion
  Of feelings or fingers or bunions or breeks,
But it hustles you some to find proper occasion
  When you have a year's weeping to do in two weeks!

Counting one evening my toes and my fingers
  I found them unchanged with the passing of years,
And I muttered, "How sad that the same number lingers!"
  And crept to my cot in a tempest of tears.

When I noted at morn that the sun was still rising
  To the eastward of things instead of the west
Its pathos so smote me 'tis scarcely surprising
  I tore at my tresses and beat on my breast.

I went to Niagara. Leaping and throbbing
  The waterfall fell, as per many an ad.
But over its roar rose the sound of my sobbing—
  The water was moister, but I was more sad!

What did I do on my blooming vacation?
  Quite often I ate and I frequently slept,
But mostly I sobbed—I think with elation
  How I wept and I wept and I wept and I wept!

Ralph Hodgson

EVE

Eve, with her basket, was
Deep in the bells and grass,
Wading in bells and grass
Up to her knees.
Picking a dish of sweet
Berries and plums to eat,
Down in the bells and grass
Under the trees.

Mute as a mouse in a
Corner the cobra lay,
Curled round a bough of the
Cinnamon tall....
Now to get even and
Humble proud heaven and
Now was the moment or
Never at all.

"Eva!" Each syllable
Light as a flower fell,
"Eva!" he whispered the
Wondering maid,
Soft as a bubble sung
Out of a linnet's lung,
Soft and most silverly
"Eva!" he said.

Picture that orchard sprite;
Eve, with her body white,
Supple and smooth to her
Slim finger tips;

Wondering, listening,
Listening, wondering,
Eve with a berry
Half-way to her lips.

Oh, had our simple Eve
Seen through the make-believe!
Had she but known the
Pretender he was!
Out of the boughs he came,
Whispering still her name,
Tumbling in twenty rings
Into the grass.

Here was the strangest pair
In the world anywhere,
Eve in the bells and grass
Kneeling, and he
Telling his story low....
Singing birds saw them go
Down the dark path to
The Blasphemous Tree.

Oh, what a clatter when
Titmouse and Jenny Wren
Saw him successful and
Taking his leave!
How the birds rated him,
How they all hated him!
How they all pitied
Poor motherless Eve!

Picture her crying
Outside in the lane,
Eve, with no dish of sweet
Berries and plums to eat,

Haunting the gate of the
Orchard in vain. . . .
Picture the lewd delight
Under the hill to-night—
"Eva!" the toast goes round,
"Eva!" again.

Harry Graham

TACT

Tho' endowed with all the virtues of a Daniel,
  With a nature free from blemishes or flaws;
Tho' combining the devotion of a spaniel
  With intelligence like Mr. Bernard Shaw's;
Tho' the noblest disposition you inherit,
  And your character with piety is pack'd,
All such qualities have very little merit
  Unaccompanied by Tact.

What is Tact? you may inquire—and very rightly—
  'Tis that mixture of good taste and *savoir faire*
Which impels us to conduct ourselves politely,
  Not to gossip, not to snigger, not to stare;
To be gay (but not facetious) at a wedding,
  At a fun'ral, sympathetic but discreet—
'Tis the art, above all else, of never treading
  Upon other people's feet.

If a neighbor has a face like a geranium,
  It is rude of you to blink or shade your eyes;
If he balances a wig upon his cranium,
  You should view it with inaudible surprise.

Ere you ridicule the tint of people's noses,
  Or their lamentable paucity of hair,
Recollect how little urchins twitted Moses,
  And were eaten by a bear! *

When residing in a house where there are lovers,
  You should don the very loudest of your suits;
And a tactful man instinctively discovers
  The necessity for wearing squeaky boots.
In your efforts to prevent a private scandal,
  Which a fashionable hostess might deplore,
You should cough, and have some trouble with the handle
  Before entering a door.

It is Tact that makes the needy cringe and grovel,
  And the rich behave like Romans when in Rome;
It is Tact that brings contentment to the hovel,
  It is Tact that carries peace into the home.
It is Tact—but why this "dam'd reiteration"
  Of a simple and indisputable fact,
Since my poem needs no further illustration
  As a masterpiece of Tact!

Franklin P. Adams

THOSE TWO BOYS

When Bill was a lad he was terribly bad.
  He worried his parents a lot;
He'd lied and he'd swear and pull little girls' hair;
  His boyhood was naught but a blot.

* Was it not Elisha?—*Editor*.
There are no rhymes for Elisha. Please use some intelligence.—H. G.

At play and in school he would fracture each rule—
  In mischief from autumn to spring;
And the villagers knew when to manhood he grew
  He would never amount to a thing.

When Jim was a child he was not very wild;
  He was known as a good little boy;
He was honest and bright and the teacher's delight—
  To his mother and father a joy.

All the neighbors were sure that his virtue'd endure,
  That his life would be free of a spot;
They were certain that Jim had a great head on him
  And that Jim would amount to a lot.

And Jim grew to manhood and honor and fame
  And bears a good name;
While Bill is shut up in a dark prison cell—
  You never can tell.

*

TO A YOUNG WOMAN ON THE *WORLD* STAFF

"Sing while you work" and be full of cheer.
  And work as the young and spry work.
"Sing while you work" if you must, my dear,
  But please don't sing while *I* work.

Sara Teasdale

THE LOOK

Strephon kissed me in the spring,
  Robin in the fall,
But Colin only looked at me
  And never kissed at all.

Strephon's kiss was lost in jest,
  Robin's lost in play,
But the kiss in Colin's eyes
  Haunts me night and day.

Louis Untermeyer

THE WISE WOMAN

His eyes grow hot, his words grow wild;
  He swears to break the mold and leave her.
She smiles at him as at a child
  That's touched with fever.

She smooths his ruffled wings, she leans
  To comfort, pamper and restore him;
And when he sulks or scowls, she preens
  His feathers for him.

He hungers after stale regrets,
  Nourished by what she offers gaily;
And all he thinks he never gets
  She feeds him daily.

He lusts for freedom; cries how long
  Must he be bound by what controlled him!
Yet he is glad the chains are strong,
  And that they hold him.

She knows he feels all this, but she
  Is far too wise to let him know it;
He needs to nurse the agony
  That suits a poet.

He laughs to see her shape his life,
  As she half-coaxes, half-commands him;
And groans it's hard to have a wife
  Who understands him.

*

DER BRIEF, DEN DU GESCHRIEBEN

Your letter does not move me
  Although the words are strong;
You say you will not love me—
  But ah, the letter's long...

Twelve pages, neat and double!
  A little essay! Why,
One never takes such trouble
  To write a mere good-bye.

                    Translated from Heine

*

FÜRCHTE NICHTS, GELIEBTE SEELE

Do not fear, my love; no danger
  Ever will approach us here;
Fear no thief or any stranger—
  See, I lock the door, my dear.

Do not fear the wind that's quarreling,
  For these walls are strong and stout;
To prevent a fire, my darling,—
  See, I blow the candle out.

Let my arms fold close and thickly
　　Here about your neck and all—
One can catch a cold so quickly
　　In the absence of a shawl.

Translated from Heine

Rupert Brooke

DUST

When the white flame in us is gone,
　　And we that lost the world's delight
Stiffen in darkness, left alone
　　To crumble in our separate night;

When your swift hair is quiet in death,
　　And through the lips corruption thrust
Has stilled the labour of my breath—
　　When we are dust, when we are dust!—

Not dead, not undesirous yet,
　　Still sentient, still unsatisfied,
We'll ride the air, and shine and flit,
　　Around the places where we died,

And dance as dust before the sun,
　　And light of foot, and unconfined,
Hurry from road to road, and run
　　About the errands of the wind.

And every mote, on earth or air,
　　Will speed and gleam, down later days,
And like a secret pilgrim fare
　　By eager and invisible ways,

Nor ever rest, nor ever lie,
  Till, beyond thinking, out of view,
One mote of all the dust that's I
  Shall meet one atom that was you.

Then in some garden hushed from wind,
  Warm in a sunset's afterglow,
The lovers in the flowers will find
  A sweet and strange unquiet grow

Upon the peace; and, past desiring,
  So high a beauty in the air,
And such a light, and such a quiring,
  And such a radiant ecstasy there,

They'll know not if it's fire, or dew,
  Or out of earth, or in the height,
Singing, or flame, or scent, or hue,
  Or two that pass, in light, to light,

Out of the garden higher, higher . . .
  But in that instant they shall learn
The shattering fury of our fire,
  And the weak passionless hearts will burn

And faint in that amazing glow,
  Until the darkness close above;
And they will know—poor fools, they'll know!—
  One moment, what it is to love.

Newman Levy

IF YOU STICK A STOCK OF LIQUOR—

If you stick a stock of liquor in your locker,
It is slick to stick a lock upon your stock,

Or some joker who is slicker's going to trick you of your
    liquor;
Though you snicker you'll feel sicker from the shock.
Be a piker though your clubmates mock and bicker,
For like brokers round a ticker they will flock
To your locker full of liquor, and your stock will vanish
    quicker
If you fail to lock your liquor with a lock.

*

CARMEN

In Spain, where the courtly Castilian hidalgo twangs lightly
    each night his romantic guitar,
Where the castanets clink on the gay piazetta, and strains of
    fandangoes are heard from afar,
There lived, I am told, a bold hussy named Carmen, a pam-
    pered young vamp full of devil and guile.
Cigarette and cigar men were smitten with Carmen; from
    near and from far men were caught with her smile.
Now one day it happened she got in a scrap and proceeded
    to beat up a girl in the shop,
Till someone suggested they have her arrested, and though
    she protested they called in a cop.
In command of the guard was a shavetail named José, a
    valiant young don with a weakness for janes,
And so great was her beauty this bold second loot he could
    not do his duty and put her in chains.
"I'm sorry, my dear, to appear to arrest you,—at best you
    are hardly much more than a kid.
If I let you go, say, there'll be some exposé. But beat it," said
    José. And beat it she did.

The scene now is changed to a strange sort of tavern—a
  hangout of gypsies, a rough kind of dive,
And Carmen, who *can* sing, is warbling and dancing, await-
  ing her date the late loot to arrive.
In comes Escamillo the toreadoro and sings his great solo
  'mid plaudits and cheers,
And when he concludes, after three or four encores, the
  gypsies depart and Don José appears.
These gypsy companions of Carmen are smugglers, the
  worst band of bandits and cut throats in Spain.
And José, we know well's A.W.O.L. Says he "Since that's
  so, well I guess I'll remain."
The gypsies depart to the heart of the mountains, and with
  them goes José who's grouchy and sore.
For Carmen, the flirt, has deserted poor José, and transferred
  her love to the toreador.
And as he sits sulking he sees Escamillo. A challenge is
  passed and they draw out their knives.
Till José, though lighter, disarms the bull fighter and near
  kills the blighter when Carmen arrives.
Now comes Micaela, Don José's young sweetheart, a nice
  looking blonde without much in her dome.
Say's she, "Do you know, kid, your ma's kinder low, kid?"
  Says José, "Let's go, kid," and follows her home.
At last we arrive at the day of the bull fight; the grand
  stand is packed and the bleachers are full;
A picturesque scene, a square near the arena, the Plaza del
  Toro or Place of the Bull.
Dark skinned senoritas with fans and mantillas, and
  haughty Castilians in festive array;
And dolled out to charm men, suspecting no harm, enters,
  last of all, Carmen to witness the fray.

But here's our friend José who seizes her bridle. A wild
  homicidal glint gleams in his eye.
He's mad and disgusted and cries out, "You've busted the
  heart that once trusted you. Wed me or die!"
Though Carmen is frightened at how this scene might end,
  I'm forced to admit she is game to the last.
She says to him "Banish the notion and vanish. *Vamos!*"
  which is Spanish for "run away fast."
A scream and a struggle! She reels and she staggers, for
  Don José's dagger's plunged deep in her breast.
No more will she flirt in her old way, that's certain. So ring
  down the curtain, poor Carmen's at rest.

*

THE BELLE OF THE BALKANS

(A Broadway Operetta)

The scene: a public square in Ruritania,
Fair Ruritania, land of gay Romance,
Where the natives have a strange and curious mania
For gathering in the public square to dance.

Amid a scene of unrestricted gaiety
They drink from cups of *papier-mâché*.
The military mingle with the laity,
And sing an opening song that goes this way:

> *"Clink, clink, we merrily drink,*
>   *Though the weather be sunny or rainier.*
> *Then we sing and we laugh as our vintage we quaff*
> *From the vines of our fair Ruritania."*

Among the local bourgeoisie and peasantry
There dwelt a maid who tended at the bar.
Of all the girls, for beauty, charm and pleasantry
Dolores was the loveliest by far.

She quite surpassed the other maidens vocally.
Her skill and grace at dancing took the prize.
But, strangely, it was not suspected locally
Dolores was their princess in disguise.

And now upon the scene in Ruritania
Arrives a gay adventurer named Cohn,
A dashing lad from Scranton, Pennsylvania,
Who greets the maid in dulcet tenor tone:

> *"Dolores, my dearest, I love you,*
> *You are the ideal of my dreams.*
> *I never knew there was someone like you,*
> *You're fairer than princess or queen.*
> *Springtime you know, dear, is ring time,*
> *So let us get married in June.*
> *Then we'll stroll down life's pathway together,*
> > *My darling,*
> *Beneath the Balkan moon."*

And now, mid cheers the king appears,
A comic chap and rowdy,
A royal clown with tilted crown
Who greets the crowd with "Howdy!"

> *"Howdy, folks! I've got some jokes.*
> *Whad'd'ye think of this?*
> *My jester has written a bran new song*
> *Called 'Jester Little Kiss.'*
> *Come bring a drink for your noble kink.*
> *Don't think that I'm complaining,*

> *But it's strange that I am always dry,*
> *Although I'm always reigning.*

"I am searching with this large imposing retinue
For my daughter who is hiding here, I learn.
Which is nothing to the hiding, I am bettin' you,
That she'll get from her old dad on her return.

"She is working in this picturesque locality
As a bar maid in a neighboring café,
An employment of debatable legality,
And unsuited to a princess, I must say.

"So my troops will search this section and vicinity—"
When, behold, from out the crowd the maid appears
Quite disguised in simulated masculinity
In the costume of The Royal Grenadiers.

> *"With a rum tum tum of the fife and drum,*
> *While the banners gaily fly.*
> *For a soldier's life is a soldier's life,*
> *Which nobody can deny."*

There, beside her, stands the gallant Pennsylvanian,
As the natives gaily quench again their thirst,
Then they all join in an anthem Ruritanian,
As the curtain quickly falls on Act the First.

Act Two. A scene of glittering aristocracy:
The Palace, filled with nobles gathered there,
Who remarkably resemble the democracy
Who were gathered in Act One about the square.

There they merrily imbibe the royal potables.
Mr. Cohn is seen commingling with the throng.
Then the king arrives and entertains the notables
With a tap dance and the chorus of a song.

"Dinah, no gal is finer,
Say that you love me true.
Boop-oop-a-doop.
Way down in Carolina, Dinah,
We'll have a love nest
Just built for two."

Now once again the plot unreels,
(With time out for performing seals)
Upon the scene with royal mien
The princess enters stately.
She sings a song and does a dance,
While Cohn, amazed, looks on askance.
"Last week I saw her wearing pants.
This mystifies me greatly.

"My dear," he cries with anguished moan,
"Oh say that you remember Cohn!
Can't you recall my face at all?
Please tell me that you know me!"
The princess says, "I quite regret
That you and I have never met."
And then they sing a love duet
Entitled "In Dahomey."

Now a telegram arrives in Ruritania
Which announces that the gallant Mr. Cohn
Has been chosen Mayor of Scranton, Pennsylvania,
By the largest vote the city's ever known.

Then the king says, "Since, in your benighted domicile
That position corresponds to duke or earl,
If, to love my child and cherish her you'll promise, I'll
Be proud to let you wed my charming girl."

Then the curtain falls upon an outburst lyrical,
As the critics rush to write their morning rave.
As they pen the words "delightfully satirical"
Mr. Gilbert does a handspring in his grave.

George S. Kaufman

ADVICE TO WORRIERS

Pray list to me a modest while;
    I fain would spill an earful:
Don't worry—cultivate a smile—
    Be always bright and cheerful.

When things are looking dour and black,
    Then *you* be blithe and hearty;
Just slap me gaily on the back—
    The life of every party.

Let naught your cheery nature spoil;
    Be always gay and chipper...
And I'll supply the boiling oil,
    If someone has a dipper.

Samuel Hoffenstein

YOUR LITTLE HANDS

Your little hands,
Your little feet,
Your little mouth—
Oh, God, how sweet!

Your little nose,
Your little ears,
Your eyes, that shed
Such little tears!

Your little voice,
So soft and kind;
Your little soul,
Your little mind!

*

IF YOU LOVE ME

If you love me, as I love you,
We'll both be friendly and untrue.

*

SOME FOLKS I KNOW

Some folks I know are always worried,
That when they die, they will be buried;
And some I know are quite elated
Because they're going to be cremated.

*

THE OCEAN SPILLS

The ocean spills upon the sands
Water with a thousand hands,
And when the water all is spilled,
The sands are dry, the ocean filled.

*

A LITTLE WHILE TO LOVE AND RAVE

A little while to love and rave
And fret and sweat and fear and hope in;
A little while to bathe and shave
And keep the organism open—
Then silence under reeds and roses,
And no more blowing of our noses.

A little while to sweat and bleed
For cheese and biscuits on a table;
A little while to spill our seed
As per directions on the label—
Then dust and wind for saint and sinner,
And no bicarb to praise our dinner.

A little while to give a maid
The things she wants to make her sadder;
A little while to make the grade
Bestrewn with gravel from the bladder—
Then weeds and grass that cows will edit,
And no more cash, and no more credit.

A little while to sleep, or lie
Suspended by some weird psychosis;
To strut, or search the wandering eye
For proof of dreaded halitosis—
Then let the process-servers find us,
Our dental bridges far behind us!

Oh, Lord, who had the right idea
To tame our pride and sex and stomachs;
Who matched our teeth with pyorrhea,
Our tallest towers with graveyard hummocks—
Accept my praises now—I'd rather
Never meet the gifted Author!

Christopher Morley

THE TRYST

According to tradition
    The place where sweethearts meet
Is meadowland and hillside,
    And not the city street.

Love lingers when you say it
    By lake and moonlight glow:
The poets all O. K. it—
    It may be better so!

And yet I keep my trysting
    In the department stores:
I always wait for Emma
    At the revolving doors.
It might dismay the poets,
    And yet it's wholly true—
My heart leaps when I know it's
    My Emma, pushing through!

It may be more romantic
    By brook or waterfall,
Yet better meet on pavements
    Than never meet at all:
I want no moon beguiling,
    No dark and bouldered shore,
When I see Emma smiling
    And twirling through the door!

A. P. Herbert

"HE DIDN'T OUGHTER..."

I never will complain of my dear husband, Mrs. Henn;
When Wilkinson is sober he's no worse than other men;
We've never had no serious unpleasantness, but there—
It's little things, I've always said, are cruellest to bear.

    Well, he didn't oughter strike me, not at meals,
        I told him of it only yesterday;
    It's little things like that a woman feels;
        Why can't he wait till dinner's cleared away?

Of course he takes a drop too much, I don't complain of that,
It's what I call the bagatelles that knocks a woman flat;
I don't begrudge the man his beer, though now and then he's
    blind,
But he doesn't seem to understand the workings of my mind.

> *Well, he didn't oughter come to bed in boots—*
>   *It's little things like that fidget me, you see;*
> *I never mind his sleeping in his suits,*
>   *But why can't he sleep in stockings, same as me?*

The first two months, I *will* say, he was everything that's
    good;
He's carried on with one or two—well, anybody would;
The lodger's wife's the latest, and I daresay she's to blame—
Well, let him have his fun, I says, but can't he play the
    game?

> *And he didn't oughter kiss her when I'm there;*
>   *A woman has her pride when all is said;*
> *It's little things are cruellest to bear—*
>   *Why can't he wait till I've gone up to bed?*

*

COALS OF FIRE

"Well, Mrs. Rogers,
    I hear you're taking lodgers—
And young enough, they say, to be your son.
    Now Rogers is away, dear,
    You're moping, I daresay, dear,
And company is pleasant if it's only just the one.

    "*No offence took,*
    I trust, where none intended?

Don't leap before you look;
  Least said, the soonest mended.
And as to what the gentleman is paying,
  Don't think it's any interest for me,
Still, I thought you'd like to know what some was saying,
  So I thought I'd tell you what was said, you see."

"Thank you, Mrs. Bubble,
    But spare yourself the trouble;
I'm sure it's very good of you to call,
    And you not very well, dear,
    It's difficult to tell, dear,
But are you quite the same since you had that nasty fall?

  "No offence took,
    I trust, where none intended?
    Don't leap before you look;
  Least said, the soonest mended.
But Alice said that you'd been hearing double
  Since Bubble threw that hammer at your head;
Of course, I know she's very thick with Bubble,
  But still, I thought I'd tell you what was said."

"Thank you, Mrs. Rogers,
    But, speaking of the lodgers,
Do you mean to have another, dear, or not?
    That's what I should do, dear.
    He'll be lonely, just with you, dear;
Though I'm sure it's very cosy with those nice new blinds
    you've got.

  "No offence took,
    I trust, where none intended?
    Don't leap before you look;
  Least said the soonest mended.

I'm sorry for the boy, and him in mourning,
  Though Mabel don't believe the wife is dead;
That Mabel says too much, I give you warning,
  But still, I thought I'd tell you what she said."

"Thank you, Mrs. Bubble.
    Now how about your trouble?
Is Bubble backing losers just the same?
    You've lost a lot of hair, dear,
    You ought to take more care, dear;
But there, he's dragged you down, dear—I don't say **you're**
  to blame.

"No offence took,
  I trust, where none intended?
    Don't leap before you look;
  Least said the soonest mended.
You'll have a cup of tea? I've got it handy.
  I daresay it's a long time since your last.
Well, Mabel said you breakfasted on brandy,
  And I'd better tell you what remarks is passed."

Edna St. Vincent Millay

THE PENITENT

I had a little Sorrow,
Born of a little Sin,
I found a room all damp with **gloom**
  And shut us all within;
And, "Little Sorrow, weep," said I,
"And, Little Sin, pray God to die,
And I upon the floor will lie
  And think how bad I've been!"

Alas for pious planning—
   It mattered not a whit!
As far as gloom went in that room,
   The lamp might have been lit!
My Little Sorrow would not weep,
My Little Sin would go to sleep—
To save my soul I could not keep
   My graceless mind on it!

So up I got in anger,
   And took a book I had,
And put a ribbon on my hair
   To please a passing lad.
And, "One thing there's no getting by—
I've been a wicked girl," said I;
"But if I can't be sorry, why,
   I might as well be glad!"

*

I, being born a woman and distressed
By all the needs and notions of my kind,
Am urged by your propinquity to find
Your person fair, and feel a certain zest
To bear your body's weight upon my breast:
So subtly is the fume of life designed,
To clarify the pulse and cloud the mind,
And leave me once again undone, possessed.
Think not for this, however, the poor treason
Of my stout blood against my staggering brain,
I shall remember you with love, or season
My scorn with pity,—let me make it plain:
I find this frenzy insufficient reason
For conversation when we meet again.

Carlton Talbott

THE SISTERS KASTEMALOFF

The evening takes them unawares,
   Oppressive is the atmosphere;
And Sonya moves to go upstairs.
   "O God!" she cries, "I can't stay here...
My heart will break, my soul will smother,
   If soon I do not learn to hate.
I'll feed the cat and go kill mother
   Before it grows too late."

Leaning her brow against the wall,
   Marya listens to the wind,
Dreaming of tropic festival
   Where clothes are not so tightly pinned.
"O God! won't someone ravish me,
   A creature caged and desolate?...
I think I'd better make some tea
   Before it grows too late."

Katya begins a minor tune,
   But breaks it off with sudden chuckles;
Then, bending like a crescent moon,
   Chews viciously her gleaming knuckles.
"I've tried to laugh, I've tried to sing,
   And now the clock is striking eight;
O God! I'd do most anything
   Before it grows too late."

They sit beside the samovar,
   And each one lights a cigarette,
And time goes on, and there they are,
   And mother isn't murdered yet.

So, night by night, in this sad room,
  The Sisters Kastemaloff wait,
Hoping to share some fearful doom
  Before it grows too late.

*

A ROYAL PICKLE

Hubbubing down the dale
Comes the great farthingale,
And the thin personage
Cooped in its satin cage
Wonders what's wrong with her
Under her stomacher.

Stopping to catch her breath,
"Oh, this will be my death!"
She whimpers piteously;—
Shocked at her idiocy,
Thus, in a pickle, seen
Outside her palanquin.

Surely well-bred is she
As any Medici;
Yet with the strain of it
And the great pain of it
Under her stomacher,
What will become of her?

"A is for Apple pie,"
Mutters Sir Pewter-eye,
Poising his chin up well
Over his picardel;
"Is it not curious
That *she* should make a fuss?"

"B is for Belly-ache,"
Answers Sir Noodleshake,
Wisely, as one would say,
Turning his nose away;
"Just a mere such-and-such
Shouldn't amount to much."

Ah, but the power and
Glory within her hand!
Ah, but her gentle birth!
All, in a moment, worth
Not what a dog would give
For her prerogative.

Susan can always go
Where the high hedges grow,
And when it pleases her,
Make herself easier;
Yet must Elizabeth
Wait, though it be her death.

Viol and clarinet
Murmur their soft regret,
And the brown shepherds stare
Open-mouthed pity where,
Hubbubing down the dale,
Goes the great farthingale.

*

THE DAY CLOSES

The day closes.
All a-tremble,
Scatterwits assemble
To pick roses;

But, hearing thunder,
They only wonder
And rub their noses.
The fool supposes
The queen is quarreling
With the king's darling.
The knave chuckles,
And cracks his knuckles,
And the king dozes.

*

Dorothy Parker

UNFORTUNATE COINCIDENCE

By the time you swear you're his,
    Shivering and sighing,
And he vows his passion is
    Infinite, undying—
Lady, make a note of this:
    One of you is lying.

*

ONE PERFECT ROSE

A single flow'r he sent me, since we met.
    All tenderly his messenger he chose;
Deep-hearted, pure, with scented dew still wet—
    One perfect rose.

I knew the language of the floweret;
    "My fragile leaves," it said, "his heart enclose."
Love long has taken for his amulet
    One perfect rose.

Why is it no one ever sent me yet
   One perfect limousine, do you suppose?
Ah no, it's always just my luck to get
   One perfect rose.

*

COMMENT

Oh, life is a glorious cycle of song,
A medley of extemporanea;
And love is a thing that can never go wrong;
And I am Marie of Roumania.

*

RÉSUMÉ

Razors pain you;
Rivers are damp;
Acids stain you;
And drugs cause cramp.
Guns aren't lawful;
Nooses give;
Gas smells awful;
You might as well live.

*

FABLE

Oh, there once was a lady, and so I've been told,
Whose lover grew weary, whose lover grew cold.
"My child," he remarked, "though our episode ends,
In the manner of men, I suggest we be friends."
And the truest of friends ever after they were—
Oh, they lied in their teeth when they told me of her!

THEY PART

And if, my friend, you'd have it end,
   There's naught to hear or tell.
But need you try to black my eye
   In wishing me farewell?

Though I admit an edgèd wit
   In woe is warranted,
May I be frank? ... Such words as "——"
   Are better left unsaid.

There's rosemary for you and me;
   But is it usual, dear,
To hire a man, and fill a van
   By way of *souvenir?*

*

THE EVENING PRIMROSE

You know the bloom, unearthly white,
That none has seen by morning light—
The tender moon, alone, may bare
Its beauty to the secret air.
Who'd venture past its dark retreat
Must kneel, for holy things and sweet.
That blossom, mystically blown,
No man may gather for his own
Nor touch it, lest it droop and fall....
Oh, I am not like that at all!

BALLADE OF UNFORTUNATE
MAMMALS

Love is sharper than stones or sticks;
  Lone as the sea, and deeper blue;
Loud in the night as a clock that ticks;
  Longer-lived than the Wandering Jew.
Show me a love was done and through,
  Tell me a kiss escaped its debt!
Son, to your death you'll pay your due—
  Women and elephants never forget.

Ever a man, alas, would mix,
  Ever a man, heigh-ho, must woo;
So he's left in the world-old fix,
  Thus is furthered the sale of rue.
Son, your chances are thin and few—
  Won't you ponder, before you're set?
Shoot if you must, but hold in view
  Women and elephants never forget.

Down from Caesar past Joynson-Hicks
  Echoes the warning, ever new:
Though they're trained to amusing tricks,
  Gentler, they, than the pigeon's coo,
Careful, son, of the cursèd two—
  Either one is a dangerous pet;
Natural history proves it true—
  Women and elephants never forget.

L'ENVOI:

Prince, a precept I'd leave for you,
  Coined in Eden, existing yet:
Skirt the parlor, and shun the zoo—
  Women and elephants never forget.

Stoddard King

COMMISSARY REPORT

Our fathers were fellows of substance and weight,
They drank when they drank, and they ate when they ate,
They made a light breakfast of flapjacks and pie,
They greeted corned beef with a ravenous cry,
Their luncheon was spareribs, with beans on the side—
    They lived free and equal,
    And what was the sequel?
They died.

The men of our era are timid with food,
Their principal ration is calories, stewed,
They start off the morning with prune flakes and bran
    And patented mannas,
    And shredded bananas—
They got a whole meal from a single tin can.
They keep a keen eye on the vitamin chart,
Affect fancy diets, and know them by heart,
They pick at their food like a wren or a chick
    For fear they'll get cancer,
    And what is the answer?
They're sick.

Aldous Huxley

MALE AND FEMALE CREATED
HE THEM

Diaphenia, drunk with sleep,
Drunk with pleasure, drunk with fatigue,
Feels her Corydon's fingers creep—
Ring-finger, middle finger, index, thumb—
Strummingly over the smooth sleek drum

Of her thorax.

           Meanwhile Händel's Gigue
Turns in Corydon's absent mind
To Yakka-Hoola.

              She can find
No difference in the thrilling touch
Of one who, now, in everything
Is God-like. "Was there ever such
Passion as ours?"

             His pianoing
Gives place to simple arithmetic's
Simplest constatations:—six
Letters in Gneiss and three in Gnu:
Luncheon to-day cost three and two;
In a year—he couldn't calculate
Three-sixty-five times thirty-eight,
Figuring with printless fingers on
Her living parchment.

              "Corydon!
I faint, faint, faint at your dear touch.
Say, is it possible . . . to love too much?"

Morris Bishop

THE TALES THE BARBERS TELL

After the day is over
   And the passers-by are rare
The lights burn low in the barber-shop
   And the shades are drawn with care
To hide the haughty barbers
   Cutting each other's hair.

And dreadful tales they whisper
   To the music of the shears,
How even the deftest razor slips
   And cleaves the client's ears;
And here is the dreadfullest story
   The seated barber hears:

"A customer came to the Parlor
   And sank in the barber's chair
As a tired child sinks in his mother's arms
   And rests and huddles there;
His beard was lank and tangled,
   And burrs were in his hair.

" 'A shave!' I heard him mutter
   In accents soft and low;
I shaved him twice; and then I said,
   'A hair-cut, sir, also?'
A red-hot towel enswathed him,
   He could not answer no.

"I used the shears and clippers,
   The whisk and air-blast too,
And then I whispered in his ear:
   'Excuse me, sir, but you
Urgently need our Special
   Egg Gasoline Shampoo.'

"I think I heard him murmur,
   I think that he agreed;
I soaped and beat and ground his head
   Till it began to bleed;
'A face massage?' His silence
   Signified, 'Proceed!'

"I cured his hair of dandruff
        With all the cures there are,
I rubbed his scalp with alcohol,
        I scrubbed his face with tar,
I singed his hair and dressed it
        With oil and vinegar.

"All of my art I lavished
        On that unworthy head;
'Rise up, rise up, go kingly forth,
        For I have done!' I said.
But never a word he answered;
        My customer was dead!"

This is the dreadful story
        That barber tells whene'er
The shades are drawn in the barber-shop
        And the midnight Mazdas flare
On the hushed and haughty barbers
        Cutting each other's hair.

*

DRINKING SONG FOR PRESENT-DAY GATHERINGS

Now all good fellows, fill the bowl, fill the bowl,
        And put a little hard stuff in it,
And take a big slug from the little brown jug,
        And another big slug in a minute;
And troll a good song and tel' a good tale,
        And have another drink, pretty quick;
Not a worry we'll know for an hour or so,
        And then we'll all be sick.

Now every good fellow, gather round, gather round,
    For every good fellow must pitch in;
Bill is mixing the gin, pouring alcohol in,
    And Joe's blending Scotch in the kitchen.
A fig for the censor who'd banish our joy!
    Who cares if he shakes his head?
We'll spend a happy hour under Bacchus's power,
    And the next three days in bed.

Then all good fellows, give a cheer, give a cheer,
    There's nothing like hootch for a chappie;
Come, hip, hip, hurray, we're so joyful and gay,
    We're all of us so gol-darn happy!
(Except the good fellows who are prone on the lawn,
    And the host, drinking healing emulsions,
While the speaker of the evening has passed out cold,
    And the toastmaster's having convulsions.)

Howard Dietz

ON THE RISING GENERATION

I've watched, with microscopic eye
    The younger generation rising.
And from my watching this is my
    Conclusion baffling and surprising:
The man who merchants for his pelf—
    The dentists, druggists, and pushcartists
Will shortly be laid on the shelf
    And all the people will be artists.

Our swarthy-cheeked and rosy-lipped
    Young maid of work has just departed
To finish up a manuscript
    That she but recently had started.

My office boy has felt the call
    To higher craftsmanship, and Yetta
The herring girl has sold her stall
    To write a comic operetta.

Each new born babe yearns to express
    Himself. At birth he feels the hunger.
This early start means quick success.
    And all our artists will be younger.
Then when we all grow up and choose
    To live by sculping, writing, painting.
Who'll sell us things like food and shoes?
    I'm cold already and I'm fainting.

Joseph T. Shipley

MEDITATION

Though we love and suffer together
We cannot judge by this;
Even a petty quarrel
Shows the abyss!
We think we're overwhelmed
In endless bliss—
But as soon as it is not
A question of a kiss,
It's rather clear our understanding ends....
If you were a man, I wonder if we'd be friends.

                            (*Translated from the French of
                                Paul Géraldy*)

Ira Gershwin

THE BABBITT AND THE BROMIDE

(From "Funny Face")

I.

A Babbitt met a Bromide on the avenue one day.
They held a conversation in their own peculiar way.
They both were solid citizens—they both had been around,
And as they spoke you clearly saw their feet were on the
  ground:

CHORUS

Hello! How are you?
Howza folks? What's new?
I'm great! That's good!
Ha! Ha! Knock wood!
Well! Well! What say?
Howya been? Nice day!
How's tricks? What's new?
That's fine! How are you?

Nice weather we are having but it gives me such a pain:
I've taken my umbrella, so of course it doesn't rain.

Heigh ho! That's life!
What's new? Howza wife?
Gotta run! Oh, my!
Olive oil! Good bye!

2.

Ten years went quickly by for both these sub-sti-an-tial men,
Then history records one day they chanced to meet again.
That they had both developed in ten years there was no
  doubt,
And so of course they had an awful lot to talk about:

CHORUS

Hello! How are you?
etc.

I'm sure I know your face, but I just can't recall your name;
Well, how've you been, old boy, you're looking just about
the same.

Heigh ho! That's life!
etc.

3.

Before they met again some twenty years they had to wait.
This time it happened up above, inside St. Peter's gate.
A harp each one was carrying and both were wearing wings,
And this is what they sang as they kept strumming on the
strings:

CHORUS

Hello! How are you?
etc.

You've grown a little stouter since I saw you last, I think.
Come up and see me sometime and we'll have a little drink.
Heigh ho! That's life!
etc.

E. B. White

A FATHER DOES HIS BEST

Said I to Lord & Taylor:
    "Hot are the summer skies,
    And my son Joe would like to go
    In a big straw hat in the year-old size.

    Have you got such a thing, for summer skies,
    A nice straw hat in the year-old size?"
Said Lord & Taylor: "No."

Said I to Saks Fifth Avenue:
    "The sunshine hurts Joe's eyes;
    He used to nap in a small white cap,
    But a big straw hat in the year-old size
    Would keep the sunshine out of his eyes.
    Have you got such a thing in the year-old size?"
Said Saks Fifth Avenue: "No."

Said I to Best & Company:
    "I think it might be wise
    When noons are red to cover Joe's head
    With a big straw hat in the year-old size.
    Can you sell me one, if you think it's wise,
    A big straw hat in the year-old size?
Said Best & Company: "No."

Said I to the infant's mother:
    "It comes as a great surprise
    That our son Joe may never go
    In a big straw hat in the year-old size.
    We had no trouble with his other supplies,
    His Pyrex bottles, his spoon for eating,
    His year-old pot and his year-old sheeting,
    His feeding bib of heavy material
    To catch the spray from the flying cereal,
        Rompers to match the color of his eyes
        In the year-old size;
    These things were bought with the greatest ease
    The stores were willing and able to please,

His bands and his year-old shirts all fit,
    His crew-neck sweater and his Arnold-Knit,
    I bought him a bear and a rubber cat,
    Yet now, when he needs a big straw hat,
        I don't know where to go.
    Doesn't it come as a great surprise
    That there's no straw hat in the year-old size
    To keep the sun from the little lad's eyes?"
Said the infant's mother: "No."

Ogden Nash

TO A SMALL BOY STANDING ON MY SHOES WHILE I AM WEARING THEM

Let's straighten this out, my little man,
And reach an agreement if we can.
I entered your door as an honored guest.
My shoes are shined and my trousers are pressed,
And I won't stretch out and read you the funnies
And I won't pretend that we're Easter bunnies.
If you must get somebody down on the floor,
What in the hell are your parents for?
I do not like the things that you say
And I hate the games that you want to play.
No matter how frightfully hard you try,
We've little in common, you and I.
The interest I take in my neighbor's nursery
Would have to grow, to be even cursory,
And I would that performing sons and nephews
Were carted away with the daily refuse,
And I hold that frolicsome daughters and nieces
Are ample excuse for breaking leases.

You may take a sock at your daddy's tummy
Or climb all over your doting mummy,
But keep your attentions to me in check
Or, sunny boy, I will wring your neck.
A happier man today I'd be
Had a visiting adult done it to me.

*

THE OYSTER

The oyster's a
Confusing suitor;
It's masc., and fem.,
And even neuter.
But whether husband,
Pal, or wife,
It leads a soothing
Sort of life.
I'd like to be
An oyster, say,
In August, June,
July, or May.

*

GENEALOGICAL REFLECTION

No McTavish
Was ever lavish.

Margaret Fishback

THIS WAY OUT

Now that it doesn't matter so much any longer,
Now that my little wings are decidedly stronger,
Now that I've ceased to regard you as wholly essential,
Now that my attitude's ceased to be so reverential,
Why must you bring your heart tardily cracking in pieces?
Why must you come with your forehead in piteous creases,
Asking me painfully why I grow colder and colder,
Begging to stake out a permanent claim on my shoulder,
Whispering wanly of love and reminding me sadly
Of days when I welcomed your casual kisses so gladly?
Darling, if I had the sense of a baby I'd let you
Continue to think that I really intend to forget you.

Elspeth

IT'S A FIB

If you are a little girl,
   I will dress you neatly.
I will teach you first of all
   How to say 'yes' sweetly.

If you are a little boy,
   I will dress you neatly.
I will teach you first of all
   How to say 'no' sweetly.

Do not listen when they say
   That your silly mother
Never to her dying day
   Knew one from the other.

Robert J. Misch

TO J. S.

My every waking hour
   Is spent in thoughts of you:
From dawn to dusk, from Jan. to Dec.,
   There's nothing else I do.

But strangely I've discovered
   A thing I never knew:
That day and night, year in, year out,
   You also think of you.

Emanuel Eisenberg

REFLECTIONS IN A HOSPITAL

Myrtle, as I lie here, wrapped in
Blankets like a Seminole,
Scarcely fit to be the captain
Of my soul,

Gazing as I do with dreamy
Languor at the bare white wall,
I am wishing you could see me,
Wan and small.

Other swains prefer to show their
Manly strength or play the fop
Or call out a proud "Hello, there!"
To a cop;

Well they know that, if you're big, you're
Sure to catch a heart in thrall;
If you have a sturdy figure,
Girls will fall.

But my handsome form and face meant
Less than nought to you, my darling.
And, altho this harsh abasement
Sets me snarling

With disgust, I yet rejoice that
I am here, despite the ache;
This is just about the choice that
You would make!

Men can never capture you, love,
When they're healthy and eupeptic.
Helpless would you have your true love—
Epileptic.

Now you'll want me, weak and dumb, too,
For I'm something to be healed.
This is what a guy must come to
Ere you yield!

Geoffrey Hellman

DYNASTIC TIFF

Oh I am the King of Siam, I am!
  With cunning I rule from Bangkok.
The King of Bagdad is a sham, a sham,
While *I* am the King of Siam. (I am.)
All others I gladly goddam. Goddam
  The worthless contemptible flock!
Oh I am the King of Siam, I am!
  With cunning I rule from Bangkok.
Oh I am the King of Bagdad, egad!
  To Hell with the King of Siam!

His ruling is merely a fad, a fad,
While *I* am the King of Bagdad, egad!
His manners, moreover, are bad, quite bad,
   What can you expect from a ham?
Oh I am the King of Bagdad, egad!
   To Hell with the King of Siam!

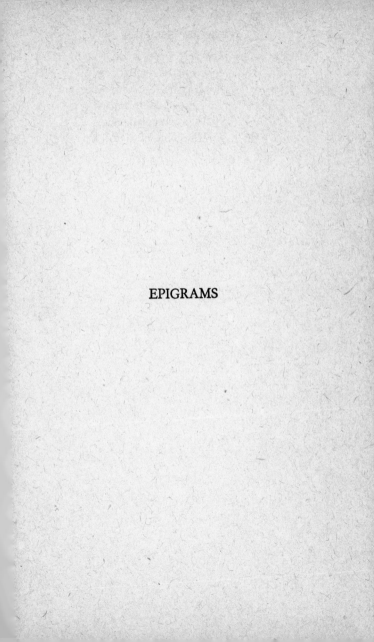

EPIGRAMS

EPIGRAMS

(If no author is assigned, the epigram in question is anonymous. As nearly as possible the verses are in chronological order.)

When the devil was sick, the devil a monk would be;
When the devil got well, the devil a monk was he.

*

TWO WENT UP TO THE TEMPLE TO PRAY

Two went to pray? O, rather say,
One went to brag, the other to pray;

One stands up close and treads on high,
Where the other dares not lend his eye;

One nearer to God's altar trod,
The other to the altar's God.

Richard Crashaw

*

OF TREASON

Treason doth never prosper; what's the reason?
For if it prosper, none dare call it treason.

Sir John Harrington

The readers and the hearers like my books,
    But yet some writers cannot them digest;
    But what care I? for when I make a feast
I would my guests should praise it, not the cooks.
                  Sir John Harrington
                  (Translated from Martial)

*

ON THE DEATH OF PYM

When lately Pym descended into hell,
    Ere he the cups of Lethe did carouse,
What place that was, he called aloud to tell;
    To whom a devil—"This is the Lower House."
            William Drummond of Hawthornden

*

ON CHARLES II

"Here lies our sovereign lord the king,
    Whose word no man relies on:
He never says a foolish thing,
    Nor ever does a wise one."
                    Lord Rochester

*

EPIGRAM

I loved thee beautiful and kind,
    And plighted an eternal vow:
So altered are thy face and mind,
    'Twere perjury to love thee now!
                Robert, Earl Nugent

The King to Oxford sent a troop of horse,
For Tories own no argument but force;
With equal skill to Cambridge books he sent,
For Whigs admit no force but argument.

Sir William Browne

*

THE WORLD

This is the best world that we live in,
To lend, and to spend, and to give in;
But to borrow, to beg, or to get a man's own,
It is the worst world that ever was known.

*

A REASONABLE AFFLICTION

On his death-bed poor Lubin lies;
    His spouse is in despair:
With frequent sobs, and mutual cries,
    They both express their care.

"A different cause," says parson Sly,
    "The same effect may give:
Poor Lubin fears that he shall die;
    His wife, that he may live."

Matthew Prior

*

To John I ow'd great obligation;
    But John unhappily thought fit
To publish it to all the nation:
    Sure John and I are more than quit.

Matthew Prior

When Pontius wished an edict might be passed
That cuckolds should into the sea be cast,
His wife, assenting, thus replied to him:
"But first, my dear, I'd have you learn to swim."

Matthew Prior (?)

*

Loud brayed an ass. Quoth Kate, "My dear,
    (To spouse, with scornful carriage)
One of your relatives I hear."
    "Yes, love," said he, "by marriage."

*

ON AN UPRIGHT JUDGE

In church your grandsire cut his throat;
To do the job too long he tarried:
He should have had my hearty vote
To cut his throat before he married.

Jonathan Swift

*

While Adam slept, from him his Eve arose:
Strange his first sleep should be his last repose.

*

I have lost my mistress, horse and wife,
And when I think of human life,
    Cry mercy 'twas no worse.
My mistress sickly, poor and old,
My wife damn'd ugly, and a scold,—
    I am sorry for my horse.

ON ONE WHO MADE LONG EPITAPHS

Friend, for your epitaphs I'm griev'd,
    Where still so much is said;
One half will never be believ'd,
    The other never read.

Alexander Pope

*

ENGRAVED ON THE COLLAR OF A DOG, WHICH I GAVE TO HIS ROYAL HIGHNESS

I am his Highness' dog at Kew;
Pray tell me, sir, whose dog are you?

Alexander Pope

*

ON THE SETTING UP MR. BUTLER'S MONUMENT IN WESTMINSTER ABBEY

While *Butler,* needy Wretch! was yet alive,
No gen'rous Patron would a Dinner give:
See him, when starv'd to Death and turn'd to Dust
Presented with a Monumental Bust!
The Poet's Fate is here in Emblem shown;
He ask'd for Bread, and he receiv'd a Stone.

Samuel Wesley

ELEGY ON COLEMAN

If heav'n be pleas'd when sinners cease to sin,
If hell be pleas'd when souls are damn'd therein,
If earth be pleas'd when it's rid of a knave,
Then all are pleas'd, for Coleman's in his grave.

*

Life is a jest; and all things show it,
I thought so once; but now I know it.

John Gay

*

ON HIS DOG

Here, Shock, the pride of all his kind, is laid,
Who fawn'd like man, but ne'er like man betray'd.

John Gay

*

Cries Sylvia to a reverend Dean,
    What reason can be given,
Since marriage is a holy thing,
    That there is none in heaven?

There are no women, he replied.
    She quick returns the jest:—
Women there are, but I'm afraid
    They cannot find a priest.

Robert Dodsley

EPITAPH ON THE LAP-DOG OF LADY FRAIL

At thieves I bark'd, at lovers wagg'd my tail,
And thus I pleased both Lord and Lady Frail.

Wilkes

*

THE MAIDEN'S CHOICE

A fool and knave with different views,
  For Julia's hand apply:
The knave, to mend his fortune, sues,
  The fool, to please his eye.

Ask you, how Julia will behave?
  Depend on't for a rule,
If she's a fool, she'll wed the knave—
  If she's a knave, the fool.

*

Cries Sue to Will, in matrimonial strife
"Cursed be the hour I first became your wife!"
"By all the powers," said Will, "but that's too bad!
You've cursed the only civil hour we've had."

*

ON THE PHRASE, "TO KILL TIME"

There's scarce a point whereon mankind agree
So well, as in their boast of killing me:
I boast of nothing, but, when I've a mind,
I think I can be even with mankind.

From the French of Voltaire

TO A POETIC LOVER:

You ask me why I have no verses sent?
For fear you should return the compliment.

W. Hay
(Translated from Martial)

*

Thou swear st thou'lt drink no more: kind heaven, send
Me such a cook, or coachman: but no such friend.

*

"No more of your titled acquaintances boast,
    And in what lordly circles you've been:
An insect is still but an insect at most,
    Though it crawl on the head of a queen!"

Robert Burns

*

A Justice walking o'er the frozen Thames,
    The ice about him round began to crack,
He said to's man, "Here is some danger, James.
    I pr'ythee help me over on thy back."

*

In Köhln, a town of monks and bones,
And pavements fanged with murderous stones,
And rags, and hags, and hideous wenches;
I counted two and seventy stenches

All well-defined and separate stinks!
Ye Nymphs that reign o'er sewers and sinks,
The river Rhine, it is well known
Doth wash your city of Cologne;
But tell me, Nymphs! what power divine
Shall henceforth wash the river Rhine?

Samuel Taylor Coleridge

*

The grateful heart for all things blesses;
    Not only joy, but grief endears:
I love you for your few caresses,
    I love you for my many tears.

Walter Savage Landor

*

Alas, how soon the hours are over
Counted us out to play the lover!
And how much narrower is the stage
Allotted us to play the sage!
But when we play the fool, how wide
The theatre expands! beside,
How long the audience sit before us:
How many prompters, what a chorus!

Walter Savage Landor

*

THE CRIMEAN HEROES

Hail, ye indomitable heroes, hail!
Despite of all your generals, ye prevail.

Walter Savage Landor

I held her hand, the pledge of bliss,
   Her hand that trembled and withdrew;
She bent her head before my kiss. . . .
   My heart was sure that hers was true.
Now I have told her I must part,
   She shakes my hand, she bids adieu,
Nor shuns the kiss. Alas, my heart!
   Hers never was the heart for you.

Walter Savage Landor

*

While life was mine, the little hour
   In drinking still unvaried flew;
I drank as earth imbibes the shower,
   Or as the rainbow drinks the dew,
As ocean quaffs the rivers up,
   Or flushing sun inhales the sea;
Silenus trembled at my cup,
   And Bacchus was out-done by me.

Thomas Moore
(After the Greek)

*

With women and apples both Paris and Adam
   Made mischief enough in their day:
God be praised that the fate of mankind, my dear madam,
   Depends not on us the same way.
For, weak as I am with temptation to grapple,
   The world would have doubly to rue thee,
Like Adam I'd gladly take from thee the apple,
   Like Paris at once give it to thee.

Thomas Moore

"Come, come," said Tom's father, "at your time of life,
There's no longer excuse for thus playing the rake—
It is time you should think, boy, of taking a wife."—
"Why, so it is, father—whose wife shall I take?"

Thomas Moore

*

ON J. W. WARD

Ward has no heart, they say; but I deny it;—
He has a heart, and gets his speeches by it.

Samuel Rogers

*

The world of fools has such a store,
That he who would not see an ass,
Must abide at home, and bolt his door,
And even break his looking-glass.

From the French

*

DEMOPHILUS

The screech-owl sings; death follows at her cries:
Demophilus strikes up; the screech-owl dies.

Henry Wellesley
(from Nicarchus)

THE BISHOP AND HIS PORTMANTEAU

"I have last my portmanteau."
  "I pity your grief."
"It contained all my sermons."
  "I pity the thief."

*

Joe hates a sycophant. It shows
Self-love is not a fault of Joe's.

*

DIVERSITY OF DOCTORS

How D.D. swaggers, M.D. rolls!
  I dub them both a brace of noddies:
Old D.D. has the cure of souls,
  And M.D. has the care of bodies.
Between them both what treatment rare
  Our souls and bodies must endure!
One has the cure without the care,
  And one the care without the cure.

*

ON TAINE

Our English critics their dull wits keep straining,
When—Enter Taine!—and all is entertaining.
                                        Alfred Ainger

I owe, says Metius, much to Colon's care;
Once only seen, he chose me for his heir:
True, Metius; hence your fortunes take their rise;
His heir you were not, had he seen you twice.

Leonard Welsted

*

Thou art in danger, Cincius, on my word,
To die ere thou hast lived, which were absurd.
Open thine ears to song, thy throat to wine,
Thy arms unto that pretty wife of thine.
Philosophy, I have nowise forgot,
Is deathless, but philosophers are not.

Richard Garnett
(From Marcus Argentarius)

*

SILENCE AND SPEECH

"I hardly ever ope my lips," one cries;
  "Simonides, what think you of my rule?"
"If you're a fool, I think you're very wise;
  If you are wise, I think you are a fool."

Richard Garnett

*

Love, like a bird, hath perched upon a spray
  For thee and me to harken what he sings.
Contented, he forgets to fly away;
  But hush! ... remind not Eros of his wings.

Sir William Watson

He is not drunk who, from the floor,
Can rise again and drink some more;
But he is drunk who prostrate lies,
And cannot drink or cannot rise.

Eugene Field

*

THE GRAMMAR OF LOVE

As Glycera was perfect, so
    Lycoris is to me,
How can the past be present, tho'
    Their futures may agree?

'Love,' 'Loved,' ah, Time's omnipotence!
    His grammar rules are crude;
By merely altering a tense
    He brings a change of mood.

Pott and Wright
(Translated from Martial)

*

TO SEXTUS

You disappoint no creditor, you say?
True, no one ever thought that you would pay.

Pott and Wright
(Translated from Martial)

They say your lady friends have no long life,
Lycoris—Let me introduce my wife.

> *Pott and Wright*
> (Translated from Martial)

*

ON LADY POLTAGRUE, A PUBLIC PERIL

The Devil, having nothing else to do,
Went off to tempt My Lady Poltagrue.
My Lady, tempted by a private whim,
To his extreme annoyance, tempted him.

> *Hilaire Belloc*

*

THE HUMORIST

He must not laugh at his own wheeze:
A snuff box has no right to sneeze.

> *Keith Preston*

*

DESTROYER

The cynic breaks stained windows
   In churches he must pass.
But he will never cast a stone
   Into a looking glass.

> *A. M. Sullivan*

PARODIES

THREE BLESSINGS

Three brightest blessings of this thirsty race,
(Whence sprung and when I don't propose to trace);
Pale brandy, potent spirit of the night,
Brisk soda, welcome when the morn is bright;
To make the third, combine the other two,
The force of nature can no further go.

Anonymous
(Dryden)

*

WHEN LOVELY WOMAN

When lovely woman wants a favor,
    And finds, too late, that man won't bend,
What earthly circumstance can save her
    From disappointment in the end?

The only way to bring him over,
    The last experiment to try,
Whether a husband or a lover,
    If he have feeling is—to cry.

Phœbe Cary
(Goldsmith)

*

THE BABY'S DÉBUT

Thy lisping prattle and thy mincing gait,
All thy false mimic fooleries I hate;
For thou art Folly's counterfeit, and she
Who is right foolish hath the better plea:
Nature's true idiot I prefer to thee.

Cumberland

*(Spoken in the character of Nancy Lake, a girl eight years
of age, who is drawn upon the stage in a child's chaise by
Samuel Hughes, her uncle's porter.)*

My brother Jack was nine in May,
And I was eight on New-year's-day;
   So in Kate Wilson's shop
Papa (he's my papa and Jack's)
Bought me, last week, a doll of wax,
   And brother Jack a top.

Jack 's in the pouts, and this it is,—
He thinks mine came to more than his;
   So to my drawer he goes,
Takes out the doll, and, O, my stars!
He pokes her head between the bars,
   And melts off half her nose!

Quite cross, a bit of string I beg,
And tie it to his peg-top's peg,
   And bang, with might and main,
Its head against the parlour-door:
Off flies the head, and hits the floor,
   And breaks a window-pane.

This made him cry with rage and spite:
Well, let him cry, it serves him right.
   A pretty thing, forsooth!

If he's to melt, all scalding hot,
Half my doll's nose, and I am not
    To draw his peg-top's tooth!

Aunt Hananh heard the window break,
And cried, 'O naughty Nancy Lake,
    Thus to distress your aunt:
No Drury Lane for you to-day!'
And while Papa said, 'Pooh, she may!'
    Mamma said, 'No, she sha'n't!'

Well, after many a sad reproach,
They got into a hackney coach,
    And trotted down the street.
I saw them go: one horse was blind,
The tails of both hung down behind,
    Their shoes were on their feet.

The chaise in which poor brother Bill
Used to be drawn to Pentonville
    Stood in the lumber-room:
I wiped the dust from off the top,
While Molly mopp'd it with a mop,
    And brush'd it with a broom.

My uncle's porter, Samuel Hughes,
Came in at six to black the shoes,
    (I always talk to Sam:)
So what does he, but takes, and drags
Me in the chaise along the flags,
    And leaves me where I am.

My father's walls are made of brick,
But not so tall and not so thick
    As these; and, goodness me!

My father's beams are made of wood,
But never, never half so good
    As those that now I see.

What a large floor! 'tis like a town!
The carpet, when they lay it down,
    Won't hide it, I'll be bound;
And there's a row of lamps!—my eye!
How they do blaze! I wonder why
    They keep them on the ground.

At first I caught hold of the wing,
And kept away; but Mr. Thing-
    umbob, the prompter man,
Gave with his hand my chaise a shove,
And said, 'Go on, my pretty love;
    'Speak to 'em, little Nan.

'You've only got to curtsy, whis-
per, hold your chin up, laugh and lisp,
    And then you're sure to take:
I've known the day when brats, not quite
Thirteen, got fifty pounds a-night;
    Then why not Nancy Lake?'

But while I'm speaking, where's papa?
And where's my aunt? and where's mamma?
    Where's Jack? O, there they sit!
They smile, they nod; I'll go my ways,
And order round poor Billy's chaise,
    To join them in the pit.

And now, good gentlefolks, I go
To join mamma, and see the show;
    So, bidding you adieu,

I curtsy, like a pretty miss,
And if you'll blow me a kiss,
    I'll blow a kiss to you.
            [*Blows a kiss, and exit.*]
                Horace and James Smith
                    (Wordsworth)

*

FRAGMENT

There is a river clear and fair,
  'Tis neither broad nor narrow;
It winds a little here and there—
It winds about like any hare;
And then it takes as straight a course
As on the turnpike road a horse,
  Or through the air an arrow.

The trees that grow upon the shore,
Have grown a hundred years or more;
  So long there is no knowing.
Old Daniel Dobson does not know
When first those trees began to grow;
But still they grew, and grew, and grew,
As if they'd nothing else to do,
  But ever to be growing.

The impulses of air and sky
Have reared their stately stems so high,
  And clothed their boughs with green;
Their leaves the dews of evening quaff,—
  And when the wind blows loud and keen,
I've seen the jolly timbers laugh,
  And shake their sides with merry glee—
  Wagging their heads in mockery.

Fix'd are their feet in solid earth,
  Where winds can never blow;
But visitings of deeper birth
  Have reached their roots below.
For they have gained the river's brink,
And of the living waters drink.

There's little Will, a five years' child—
  He is my youngest boy;
To look on eyes so fair and wild,
  It is a very joy:—
He hath conversed with sun and shower,
And dwelt with every idle flower,
  As fresh and gay as them.
He loiters with the briar rose,—
The bluebells are his play-fellows,
  That dance upon their slender stem.

And I have said, my little Will,
Why should not he continue still
  A thing of Nature's rearing?
A thing beyond the world's control—
A living vegetable soul,—
  No human sorrow fearing.

It were a blessed sight to see
That child become a willow-tree,
  His brother trees among.
He'd be four times as tall as me,
  And live three times as long.

                    Catherine Maria Fanshaw
                    (Wordsworth)

YOU ARE OLD, FATHER WILLIAM

"You are old, father William," the young man said,
  "And your hair has become very white;
And yet you incessantly stand on your head—
  Do you think, at your age, it is right?"

"In my youth," father William replied to his son,
  "I feared it would injure the brain;
But now that I'm perfectly sure I have none,
  Why, I do it again and again."

"You are old," said the youth, "as I mentioned before,
  And have grown most uncommonly fat;
Yet you turned a back somersault in at the door—
  Pray, what is the reason for that?"

"In my youth," said the sage as he shook his grey locks,
  "I kept all my limbs very supple
By the use of this ointment—one shilling the box—
  Allow me to sell you a couple."

"You are old," said the youth, "and your jaws are too weak
  For anything stronger than suet;
Yet you finished the goose, with the bones and the beak:
  Pray, how did you manage to do it?"

"In my youth," said his father, "I took to the law,
  And argued each case with my wife;
And the muscular strength, which it gave to my jaw,
  Has lasted the rest of my life."

"You are old," said the youth, "one would hardly suppose
  That your eye was as steady as ever;
Yet you balanced an eel on the end of your nose—
  What made you so awfully clever?"

"I have answered three questions, and that is enough,"
    Said his father; "don't give yourself airs!
Do you think I can listen all day to such stuff?
    Be off, or I'll kick you downstairs!"

Lewis Carroll
(Southey)

*

OZYMANDIAS REVISITED

I met a traveller from an antique land
Who said: Two vast and trunkless legs of stone
Stand in the desert. Near them on the sand,
Half sunk, a shatter'd visage lies, whose frown
And wrinkled lip and sneer of cold command
Tell that its sculptor well those passions read
Which yet survive, stamp'd on these lifeless things,
The hand that mocked them and the heart that fed;
And on the pedestal these words appear:
'My name is Ozymandias, king of kings!
Look on my works, ye Mighty, and despair!'
Also the names of Emory P. Gray,
Mr. and Mrs. Dukes, and Oscar Baer,
Of 17 West 4th Street, Oyster Bay.

Morris Bishop
(Shelley)

*

Source immaterial of material naught,
    Focus of light infinitesimal,
Sum of all things by sleepless Nature wrought,
    Of which the normal man is decimal.

Refract, in Prism immortal, from thy stars
　　To the stars bent incipient on our flag,
The beam translucent, neutrifying death,
　　And raise to immortality the rag.
　　　　　　　　　　Robert Henry Newell
　　　　　　　　　　　(Emerson)

*

"THE DAY IS DONE"

The day is done, and darkness
　　From the wing of night is loosed,
As a feather is wafted downward,
　　From a chicken going to roost.

I see the lights of the baker,
　　Gleam through the rain and mist,
And a feeling of sadness comes o'er me,
　　That I cannot well resist.

A feeling of sadness and longing
　　That is not like being sick,
And resembles sorrow only
　　As a brickbat resembles a brick.

Come, get for me some supper,—
　　A good and regular meal—
That shall soothe this restless feeling,
　　And banish the pain I feel.

Not from the pastry bakers,
　　Not from the shops for cake;
I would n't give a farthing
　　For all that they can make.

For, like the soup at dinner,
   Such things would but suggest
Some dishes more substantial,
   And to-night I want the best.

Go to some honest butcher,
   Whose beef is fresh and nice,
As any they have in the city,
   And get a liberal slice.

Such things through days of labor,
   And nights devoid of ease,
For sad and desperate feelings,
   Are wonderful remedies.

They have an astonishing power
   To aid and reinforce,
And come like the "finally, brethren,"
   That follows a long discourse.

Then get me a tender sirloin
   From off the bench or hook.
And lend to its sterling goodness
   The science of the cook.

And the night shall be filled with comfort,
   And the cares with which it begun
Shall fold up their blankets like Indians,
   And silently cut and run.

Phœbe Cary
(Longfellow)

THE HIGHER PANTHEISM IN A NUTSHELL

One, who is not, we see: but one, whom we see not, is;
Surely this is not that: but that is assuredly this.

What, and wherefore, and whence? for under is over and
    under;
If thunder could be without lightning, lightning could be
    without thunder.

Doubt is faith in the main: but faith, on the whole, is doubt;
We cannot believe by proof: but could we believe without?

Why, and whither, and how? for barley and rye are not
    clover;
Neither are straight lines curves: yet over is under and over.

Two and two may be four: but four and four are not eight;
Fate and God may be twain: but God is the same thing as
    fate.

Ask a man what he thinks, and get from a man what he
    feels;
God, once caught in the fact, shews you a fair pair of heels.

Body and spirit are twins: God only knows which is which;
The soul squats down in the flesh, like a tinker drunk in a
    ditch.

One and two are not one: but one and nothing is two;
Truth can hardly be false, if falsehood cannot be true.

Once the mastodon was: pterodactyls were common as cocks;
Then the mammoth was God: now is He a prize ox.

Parallels all things are: yet many of these are askew.
You are certainly I: but certainly I am not you.

Springs the rock from the plain, shoots the stream from the
    rock;
Cocks exist for the hen: but hens exist for the cock.

God, whom we see not, is: and God, who is not, we see;
Fiddle, we know, is diddle: and diddle, we take it, is dee.

Algernon Charles Swinburne
(Tennyson)

*

THE COCK AND THE BULL

You see this pebble-stone? It's a thing I bought
Of a bit of a chit of a boy i' the mid o' the day—
I like to dock the smaller parts-o'-speech,
As we curtail the already cur-tail'd cur
(You catch the paronomasia, play 'po' words?)
Did, rather, i' the pre-Landseerian days.
Well, to my muttons. I purchased the concern,
And clapt it i' my poke, having given for same
By way o' chop, swop, barter or exchange—
"Chop" was my snickering dandiprat's own term—
One shilling and fourpence, current coin o' the realm.
O-n-e one and f-o-u-r four
Pence, one and fourpence—you are with me, sir?—
What hour it skills not: ten or eleven o' the clock,
One day (and what a roaring day it was
Go shop or sight-see—bar a spit o' rain!)
In February, eighteen sixty nine,
Alexandrina Victoria, Fidei
Hm—hm—how runs the jargon? being on throne.

Such, sir, are all the facts, succinctly put,
The basis or substratum—what you will—
Of the impending eighty thousand lines.
"Not much in 'em either," quoth perhaps simple Hodge.
But there's a superstructure. Wait a bit.

Mark first the rationale of the thing:
Hear logic rivel and levigate the deed.
That shilling—and for matter o' that, the pence—
I had o' course upo' me—wi' me say—
(*Mecum* 's the Latin, make a note o' that)
When I popp'd pen i' stand, scratch'd ear, wiped snout,
(Let everybody wipe his own himself)
Sniff'd—tch!—at snuffbox; tumbled up, he-heed,
Haw-haw'd (not hee-haw'd, that another guess thing:)
Then fumbled at, and stumbled out of, door,
I shoved the timber ope wi' my omoplat;
And *in vestibulo,* i' the lobby to-wit,
(Iacobi Facciolati's rendering, sir,)
Donn'd galligaskins, antigropeloes,
And so forth; and, complete with hat and gloves,
One on and one a-dangle i' my hand,
And ombrifuge (Lord love you!), case o' rain,
I flopp'd forth, 'sbubbikins! on my own ten toes,
(I do assure you there be ten of them),
And went clump-clumping up hill and down dale
To find myself o' the sudden i' front o' the boy.
Put case I hadn't 'em on me, could I ha' bought
This sort-o'-kind-o'-what-you-might-call toy,
This pebble-thing, o' the boy-thing? Q. E. D.
That's proven without aid from mumping Pope,
Sleek porporate or bloated Cardinal.
(Isn't it, old Fatchaps? You're in Euclid now.)

So, having the shilling—having i' fact a lot—
And pence and halfpence, ever so many o' them,
I purchased, as I think I said before,
The pebble (*lapis, lapidis, -di, -dem, -de*—
What nouns 'crease short i' the genitive, Fatchaps, eh?)
O' the boy, a bare-legg'd beggarly son of a gun,
For one-and-fourpence. Here we are again.

Now Law steps in, bigwigg'd voluminous-jaw'd;
Investigates and re-investigates.
Was the transaction illegal? Law shakes head.
Perpend, sir, all the bearings of the case.

At first the coin was mine, the chattel his.
But now (by virtue of the said exchange
And barter) *vice versa* all the coin,
Per juris operationem, vests
I' the boy and his assigns till ding o' doom;
(*In sæcula sæculo-o-o-orum;*
I think I hear the Abate mouth out that.)
To have and hold the same to him and them...
Confer some idiot on Conveyancing.
Whereas the pebble and every part thereof,
And all that appertaineth thereunto,
Quodcunque pertinet ad eam rem,
(I fancy, sir, my Latin's rather pat)
Or shall, will, may, might, can, could, would or should.
(*Subaudi cætera*—clap we to the close—
For what's the good of law in a case o' the kind)
Is mine to all intents and purposes.
This settled, I resume the thread o' the tale.

Now for a touch o' the vendor's quality.
He says a gen'lman bought a pebble of him,
(This pebble i' sooth, sir, which I hold i' my hand)—

And paid for't, *like* a gen'lman, on the nail.
"Did I o'ercharge him a ha'penny? Devil a bit.
Fiddlepin's end! Get out, you blazing ass!
Gabble o' the goose. Don't bugaboo-baby *me!*
Go double or quits? Yah! tittup! what's the odds?"
—There's the transaction view'd i' the vendor's light.

   Next ask that dumpled hag, stood snuffling by,
With her three frowsy blowsy brats o' babes,
The scum o' the kennel, cream o' the filth-heap—Faugh!
Aie, ai, aie, aie! ὀτοτοτοτοτοῖ,
('Stead which we blurt out Hoighty toighty now)—
And the baker and candlestickmaker, and Jack and Gill,
Blear'd Goody this and queasy Gaffer that.
Ask the schoolmaster. Take schoolmaster first.

   He saw a gentleman purchase of a lad
A stone, and pay for it *rite,* on the square,
And carry it off *per saltum,* jauntily,
Propria quæ maribus, gentleman's property now
(Agreeably to the law explain'd above),
In proprium usum, for his private ends.
The boy he chuck'd a brown i' the air, and bit
I' the face the shilling: heaved a thumping stone
At a lean hen that ran cluck clucking by,
(And hit her, dead as nail i' post o' door,)
Then *abiit*—what's the Ciceronian phrase?—
Excessit, evasit, erupit—off slogs boy;
Off like bird, *avi similis*—(you observed
The dative? Pretty i' the Mantuan!)—*Anglice*
Off in three flea skips. *Hactenus,* so far,
So good, *tam bene. Bene, satis, male*—,
Where was I with my trope 'bout one in a quag?
I did once hitch the syntax into verse:

Verbum personale, a verb personal,
Concordat—ay, "agrees," old Fatchaps—*cum*
Nominativo, with its nominative,
Genere, i' point o' gender, *numero,*
O' number, *et persona,* and person. *Ut,*
Instance: *Sol ruit,* down flops sun, *et* and,
Montes umbrantur, out flounce mountains. Pah!
Excuse me, sir, I think I'm going mad.
You see the trick on't though, and can yourself
Continue the discourse *ad libitum.*
It takes up about eighty thousand lines,
A thing imagination boggles at:
And might, odds-bobs, sir! in judicious hands
Extend from here to Mesopotamy.

Charles Stuart Calverley
(Browning)

*

LARRY O'TOOLE

You've all heard of Larry O'Toole,
Of the beautiful town of Drumgoole;
 He had but one eye,
 To ogle ye by—
Oh, murther, but that was a jew'l!
  A fool
He made of de girls, did O'Toole.

'Twas he was the boy didn't fail,
That tuck down pataties and mail;
 He never would shrink
 From any sthrong dhrink,

Was it whiskey or Drogheda ale;
> I'm bail
This Larry would swallow a pail.

Oh, many a night at the bowl,
With Larry I've sot cheek by jowl;
> He's gone to his rest,
> Where there's dhrink of the best,
And so let us give his old sowl
> A howl,
For 'twas he made the noggin to rowl.

> *William Makepeace Thackeray*
> (Lever)

*

IN THE GLOAMING

In the Gloaming to be roaming, where the crested waves are
> foaming,
> And the shy mermaidens combing locks that ripple to their
> feet;
When the Gloaming is, I never made the ghost of an en-
> deavour
> To discover—but whatever were the hour, it would be
> sweet.

"To their feet," I say, for Leech's sketch indisputably teaches
> That the mermaids of our beaches do not end in ugly tails,
Nor have homes among the corals; but are shod with neat
> balmorals,
> An arrangement no one quarrels with, as many might with
> scales.

Sweet to roam beneath a shady cliff, of course with some
  young lady,
 Lalage, Neæra, Haidee, or Elaine, or Mary Ann:
Love, you dear delusive dream, you! Very sweet your victims
  deem you,
 When, heard only by the seamew, they talk all the stuff
  one can.

Sweet to haste, a licensed lover, to Miss Pinkerton the glover,
 Having managed to discover what is dear Neæra's "size":
P'raps to touch that wrist so slender, as your tiny gift you
  tender,
 And to read you're no offender, in those laughing hazel
  eyes.

Then to hear her call you "Harry," when she makes you
  fetch and carry—
 O young men about to marry, what a blessed thing it is!
To be photograph'd—together—cased in pretty Russia
  leather—
 Hear her gravely doubting whether they have spoilt your
  honest phiz!

Then to bring your plighted fair one first a ring—a rich and
  rare one—
 Next a bracelet, if she'll wear one, and a heap of things
  beside;
And serenely bending o'er her, to inquire if it would bore her
 To say when her own adorer may aspire to call her bride!

Then, the days of courtship over, with your WIFE to start for
  Dover
 Or Dieppe—and live in clover evermore, what'er befalls:

For I've read in many a novel that, unless they've souls that
   grovel,
   Folks *prefer* in fact a hovel to your dreary marble halls:

To sit, happy married lovers; Phillis trifling with a plover's
   Egg, while Corydon uncovers with a grace the Sally Lunn,
Or dissects the lucky pheasant—that, I think, were passing
   pleasant;
   As I sit alone at present, dreaming darkly of a Dun.

Charles Stuart Calverley
(Elizabeth Barrett Browning)

*

SALAD

O cool in the summer is salad,
   And warm in the winter is love;
And a poet shall sing you a ballad
   Delicious thereon and thereof.
A singer am I, if no sinner,
   My Muse has a marvellous wing,
And I willingly worship at dinner
      The Sirens of Spring.

Take endive...like love it is bitter;
   Take beet...for like love it is red;
Crisp leaf of the lettuce shall glitter,
   And cress from the rivulet's bed;
Anchovies foam-born, like the Lady
   Whose beauty has maddened this bard;
And olives, from groves that are shady;
      And eggs—boil 'em hard.

Mortimer Collins
(Swinburne)

ATALANTA IN CAMDEN-TOWN (1867)

Ay, 'twas here, on this spot,
  In that summer of yore,
Atalanta did not
  Vote my presence a bore,
Nor reply to my tenderest talk "She had heard all that non-
    sense before."

She'd the brooch I had bought her
  And the necklace and sash on,
And her heart, as I thought,
  Was alive to my passion;
And she'd done up her hair in the style that the Empress
    had brought into fashion.

I had been to the play
  With my pearl of a Peri—
But, for all I could say,
  She declared she was weary,
That "the place was so crowded and hot, and she couldn't
    abide that Dundreary."

Then I thought "Lucky boy!
  'Tis for *you* that she whimpers!"
And I noted with joy
  Those sensational simpers:
And I said "This is scrumptious!"—a phrase I had learned
    from the Devonshire shrimpers.

And I vowed " 'Twill be said
  I'm a fortunate fellow,
When the breakfast is spread,
  When the topers are mellow,
When the foam of the bride-cake is white, and the fierce
    orange-blossoms are yellow!"

O that languishing yawn!
　　O those eloquent eyes!
I was drunk with the dawn
　　Of a splendid surmise—
I was stung by a look, I was slain by a tear, by a tempest
　　of sighs.

　Then I whispered "I see
　　The sweet secret thou keepest,
And the yearning for *ME*
　　That thou wistfully weepest!
And the question is 'License or Banns?', though undoubt-
　　edly Banns are the cheapest."

　"Be my Hero," said I,
　　"And let *me* be Leander!"
But I lost her reply—
　　Something ending with "gander"—
For the omnibus rattled so loud that no mortal could quite
　　understand her.

Lewis Carroll
(Swinburne)

*

NEPHELIDIA

From the depth of the dreamy decline of the dawn through
　　a notable nimbus of nebulous moonshine,
　Pallid and pink as the palm of the flag-flower that flickers
　　with fear of the flies as they float,
Are they looks of our lovers that lustrously lean from a
　　marvel of mystic miraculous moonshine,
　These that we feel in the blood of our blushes that thicken
　　and threaten with throbs through the throat?

Thicken and thrill as a theatre thronged at appeal of an
    actor's appalled agitation,
    Fainter with fear of the fires of the future than pale with
      the promise of pride in the past;
Flushed with the famishing fulness of fever that reddens
    with radiance of rathe recreation,
    Gaunt as the ghastliest of glimpses that gleam through
      the gloom of the gloaming when ghosts go aghast?
Nay, for the nick of the tick of the time is a tremulous touch
    on the temples of terror,
    Strained as the sinews yet strenuous with strife of the dead
      who is dumb as the dust-heaps of death;
Surely no soul is it, sweet as the spasm of erotic emotional
    exquisite error,
    Bathed in the balms of beatified bliss, beatific itself by
      beatitude's breath.
Surely no spirit or sense of a soul that was soft to the spirit
    and soul of our senses
    Sweetens the stress of surprising suspicion that sobs in the
      semblance and sound of a sigh;
Only this oracle opens Olympian, in mystical moods and
    triangular tenses,—
    "Life is the lust of a lamp for the light that is dark till the
      dawn of the day when we die."
Mild is the mirk and monotonous music of memory, melodi-
    ously mute as it may be,
    While the hope in the heart of a hero is bruised by the
      breach of men's rapiers, resigned to the rod;
Made meek as a mother whose bosom-beats bound with the
    bliss-bringing bulk of a balm-breathing baby,
    As they grope through the grave-yard of creeds, under
      skies growing green at a groan for the grimness of
      God.

Blank is the book of his bounty beholden of old, and its bind-
 ing is blacker than bluer:
  Out of blue into black is the scheme of the skies, and their
   dews are the wine of the bloodshed of things;
Till the darkling desire of delight shall be free as a fawn
 that is freed from the fangs that pursue her,
  Till the heart-beats of hell shall be hushed by a hymn from
   the hunt that has harried the kennel of kings.

Algernon Charles Swinburne
(Swinburne)

*

REMEMBER

Remember it, although you're far away—
 Too far away more fivers yet to land,
  When you no more can proffer notes of hand,
Nor I half yearn to change my yea to nay.
Remember, when no more in airy way,
 You tell me of repayment sagely planned:
  Only remember it, you understand!
It's rather late to counsel you to pay;
Yet if you should remember for a while,
 And then forget it wholly, I should grieve;
  For, though your light procrastinations leave
  Small remnants of the hope that once I had,
Than that you should forget your debt and smile,
 I'd rather you'd remember and be sad.

Judy
(Christina Rossetti)

OWEN SEAMAN

WITH A GENUFLECTION TO GUY WETMORE CARRYL, TELLS THE
TALE OF "SPRATT VS. SPRATT"

Of all of the gruesome attempts at a twosome
   The worst of the lot were the Spratts;
Their life was a series of quibbles and queries,
   And quarrels and squabbles and spats.
They argued at breakfast, they argued at tea,
And they argued from midnight till quarter past three.[1]

The paterfamilias was rather a silly ass
   With an appetite passing belief;
A garrulous glutton, he ate up the mutton,
   The chicken, the chops and the beef.
His dining-room manner was almost obscene:
He threw his wife fat while *he* gobbled the lean!

He railed at her reading, her brain and her breeding,
   Her goodness, her glands and her girth;
He mentioned with loathing the state of her clothing
   And also the State of her birth.[2]
But his malice exceeded all bounds of control
When he scoffed at her Art and the state of her Soul.

To show her what home meant he gave her no moment
   Of leisure, not even at night.
He bellowed, "I'll teach ye to read Shaw and Nietzsche,"
   And quoted from Harold Bell Wright.
"The place for a woman—" he'd start, very glib...
And so on for two or three hours *ad lib.*[3]

  [1] A.M.
  [2] Oklahoma.
  [3] Also *ad nauseam.*

So very malignant became his indignant
   Remarks about "culture" and "cranks,"
That at last she revolted: she upped and she bolted
   And died in the radical ranks.

.   .   .   .   .   .

Her will left him silent in a pique up in Darien [4]
When he found she had founded *The New Vegetarian*. [5]

And *The Moral* is this (though a bit obstruse):
What's sauce for a more or less proper goose,
When it rouses the violent feminine dander,
Is apt to be sauce for the propaganda!

                             Louis Untermeyer

[4] Connecticut.
[5] *A Monthly Magazine or Moral Masticators.*

INDEX OF AUTHORS

#29886